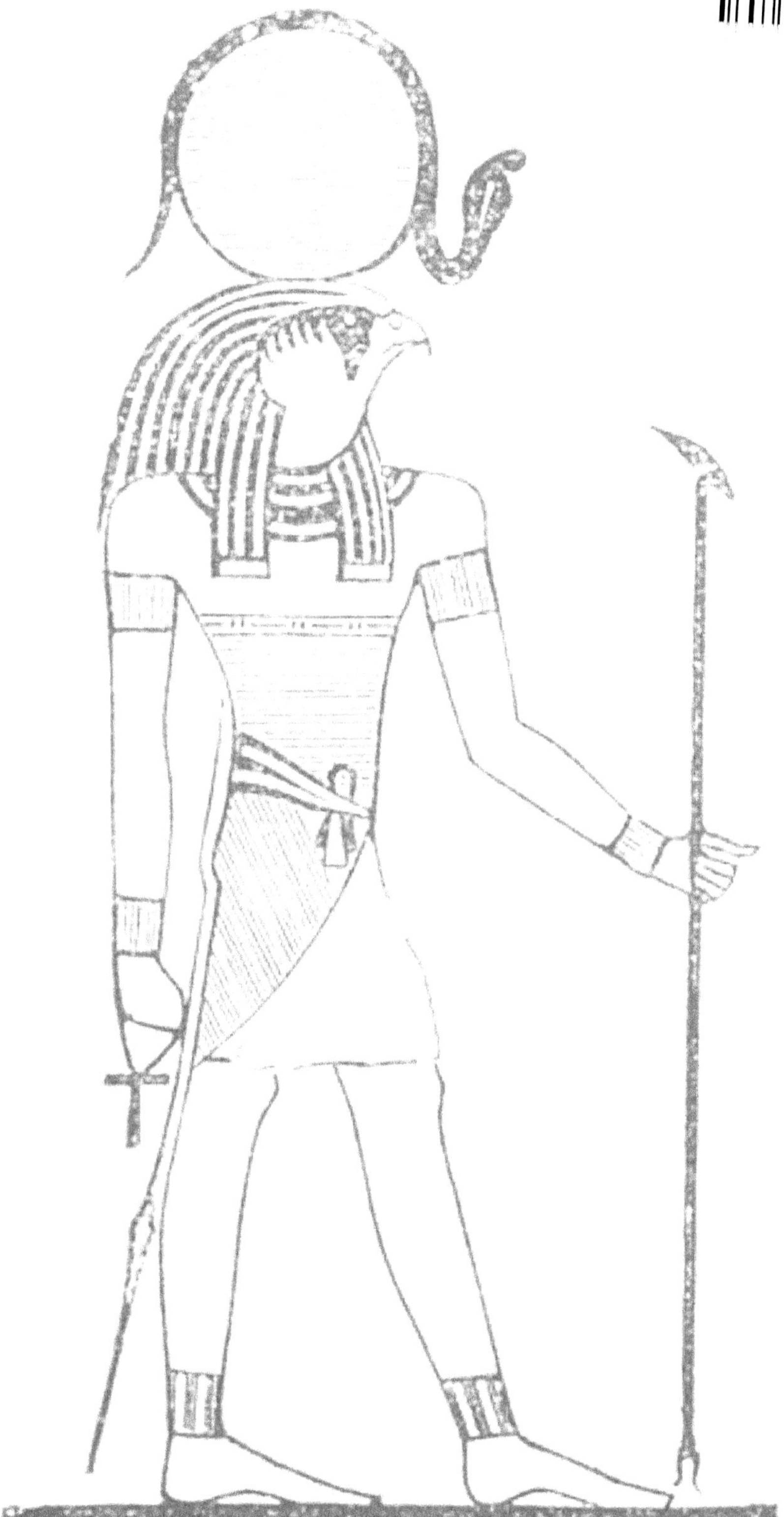

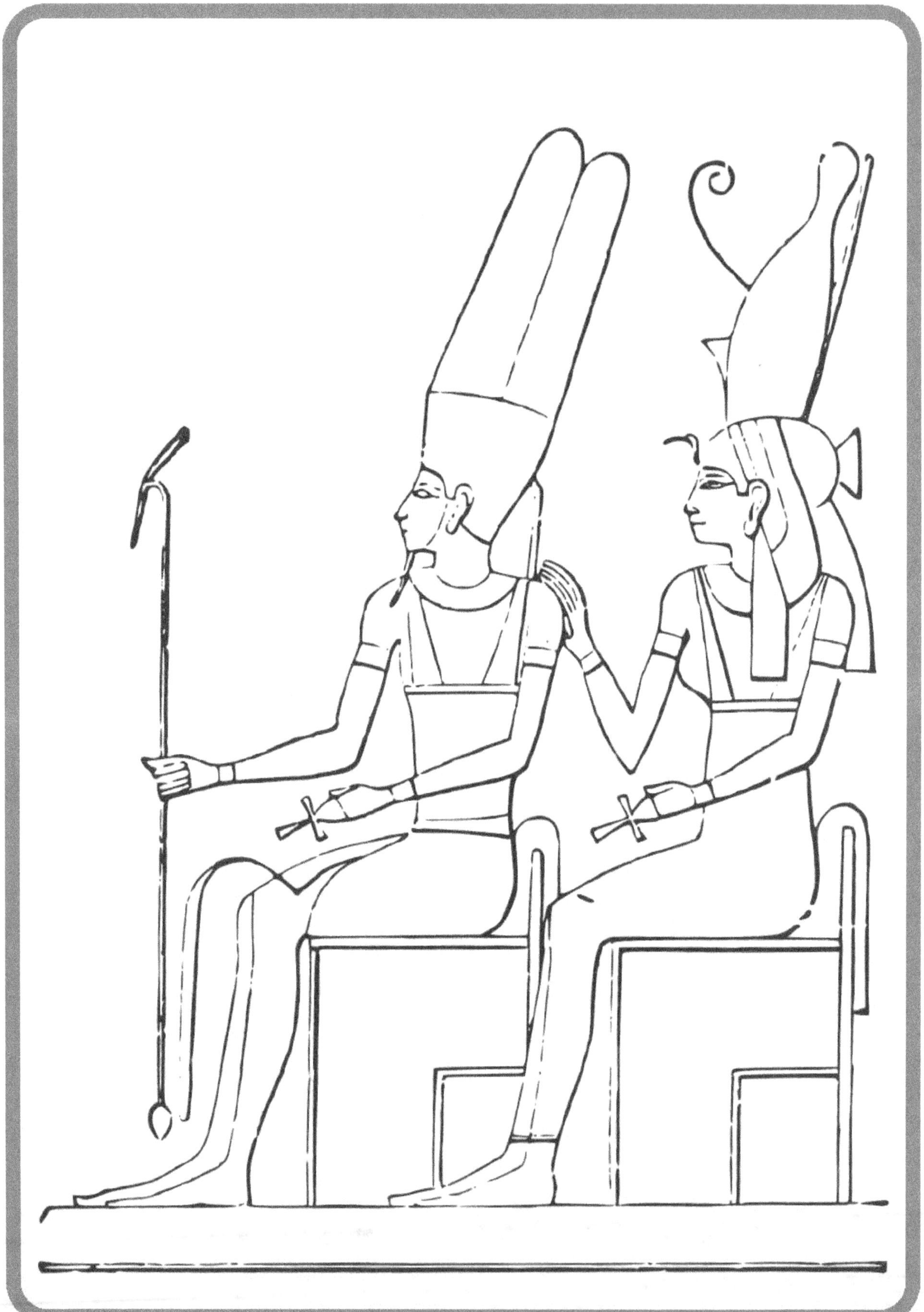

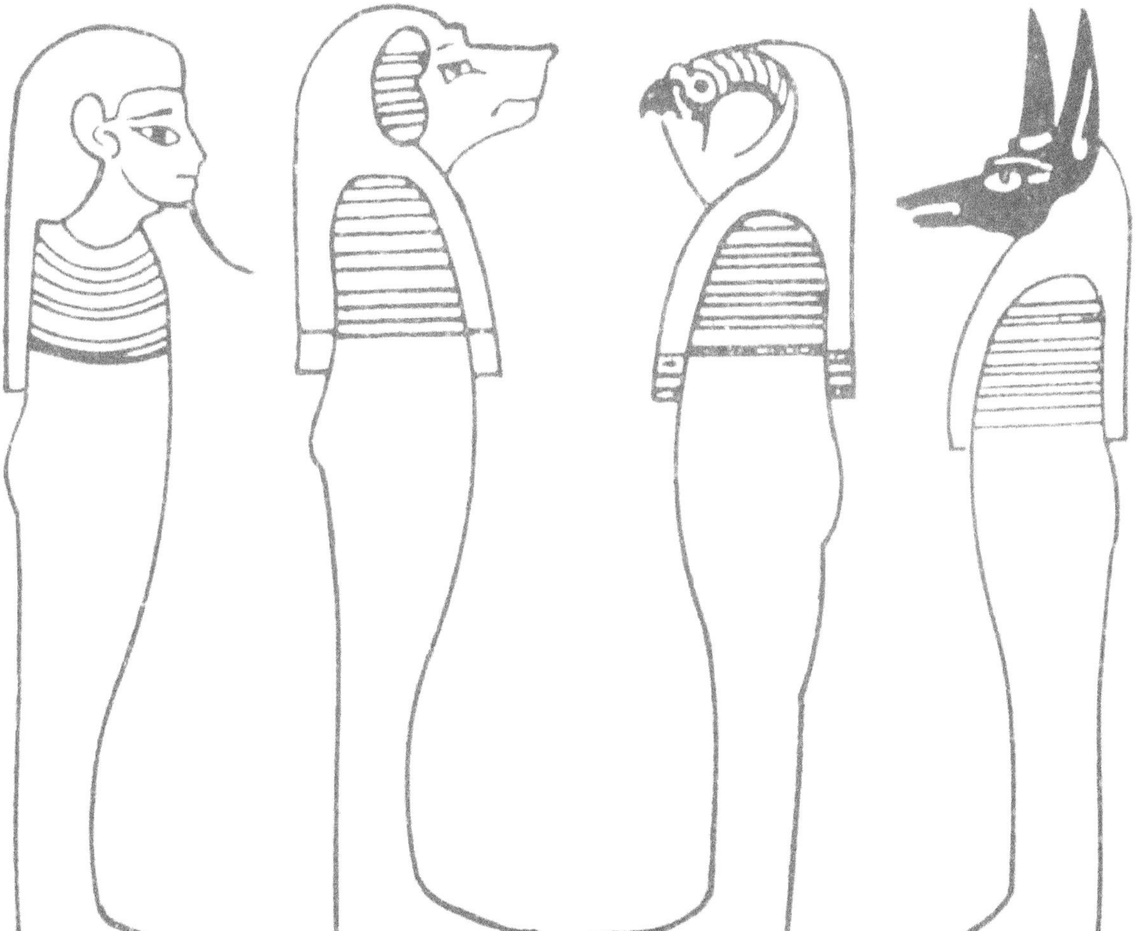
Mestha.
Hapi.
Tuamutef.
Qebhsennuf.

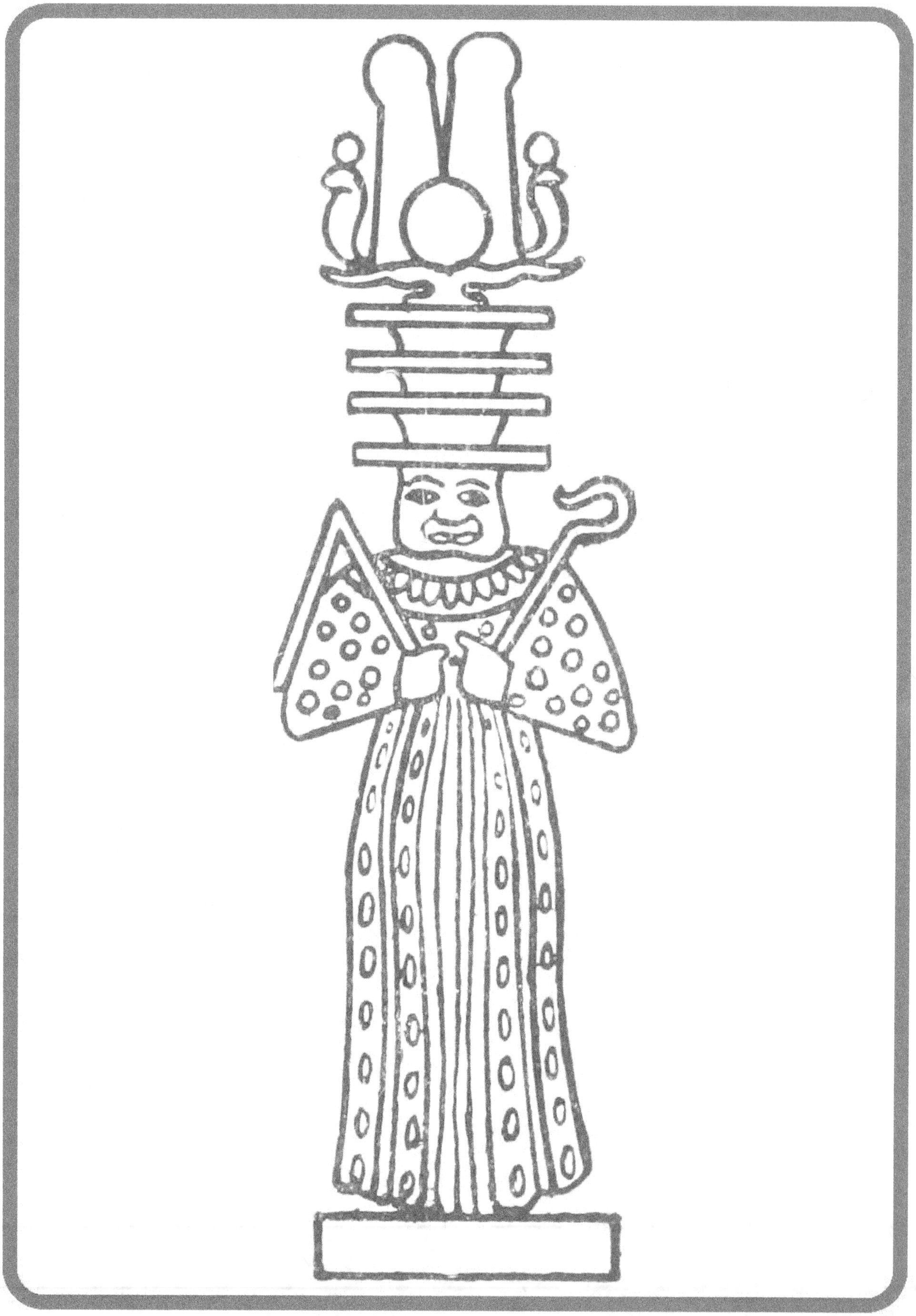

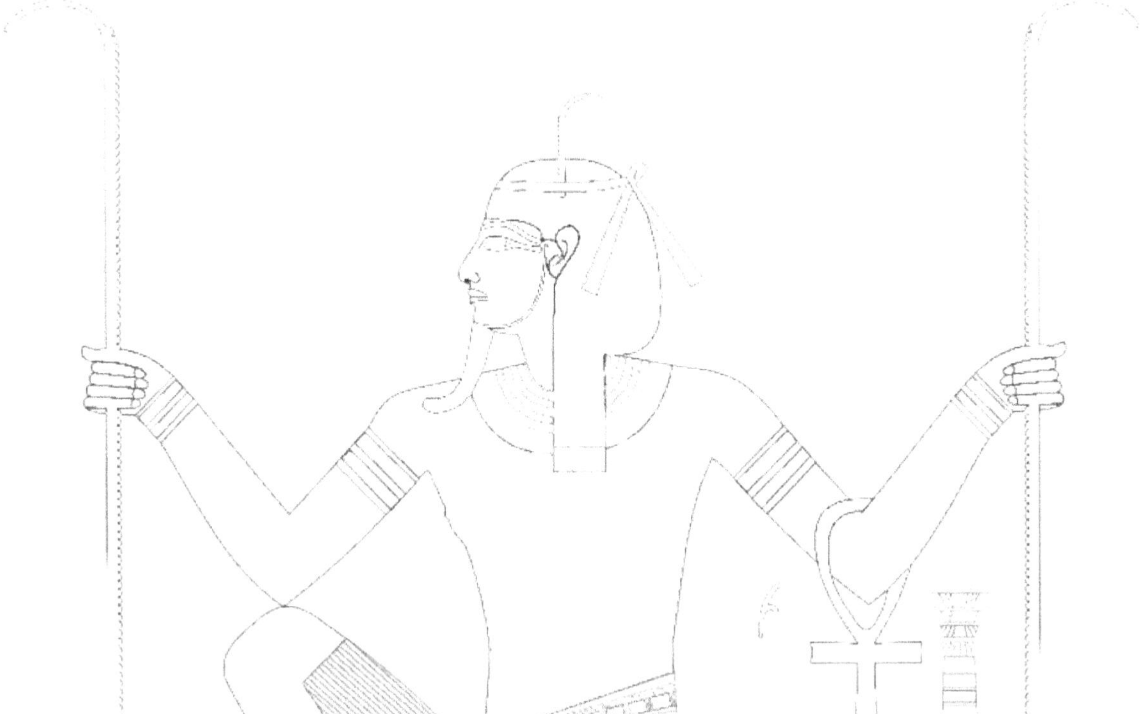

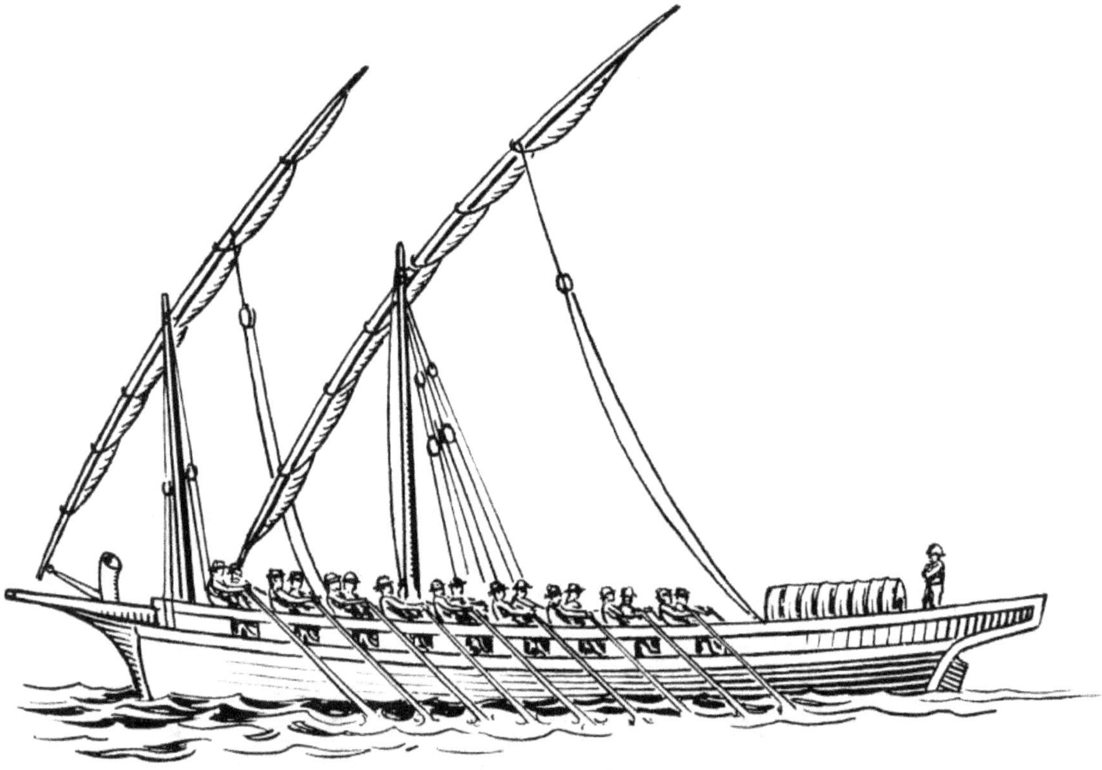

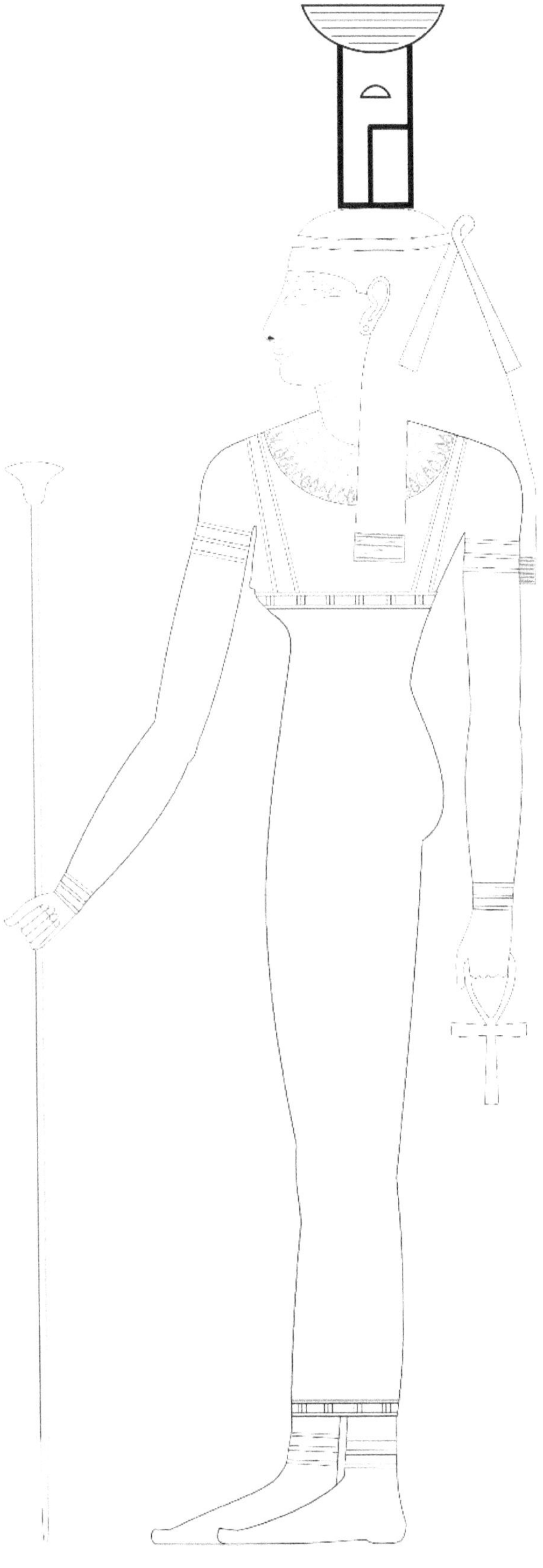

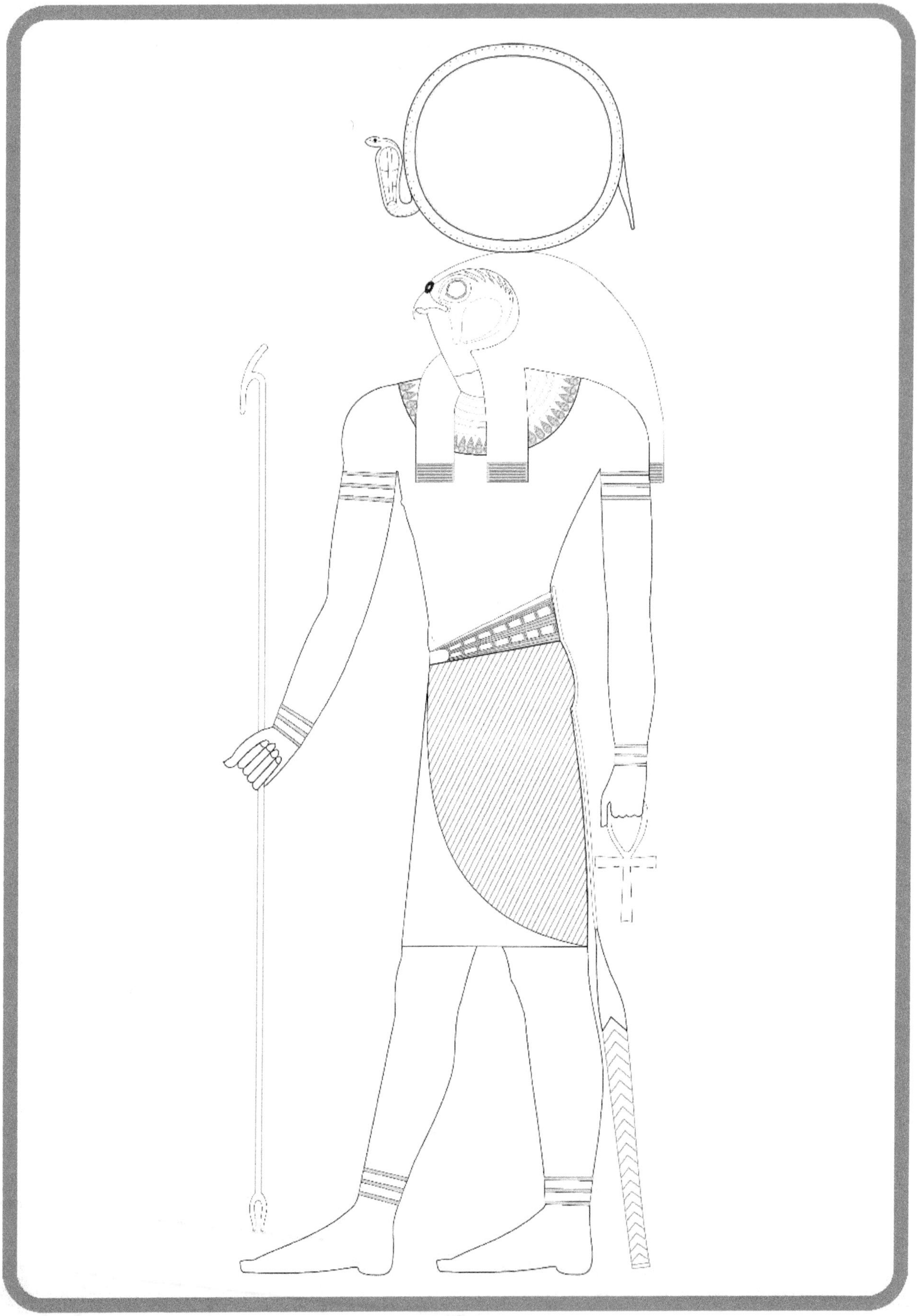

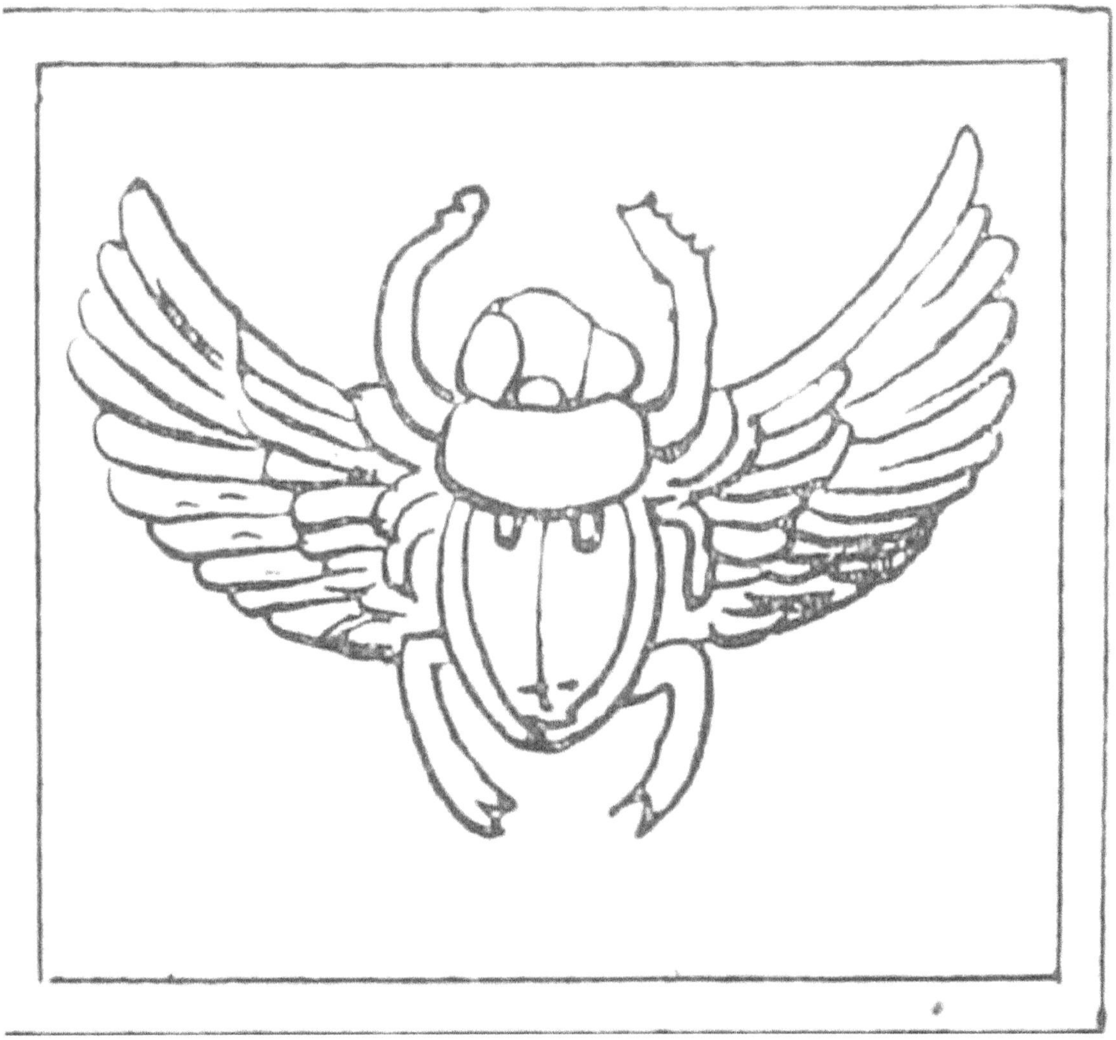

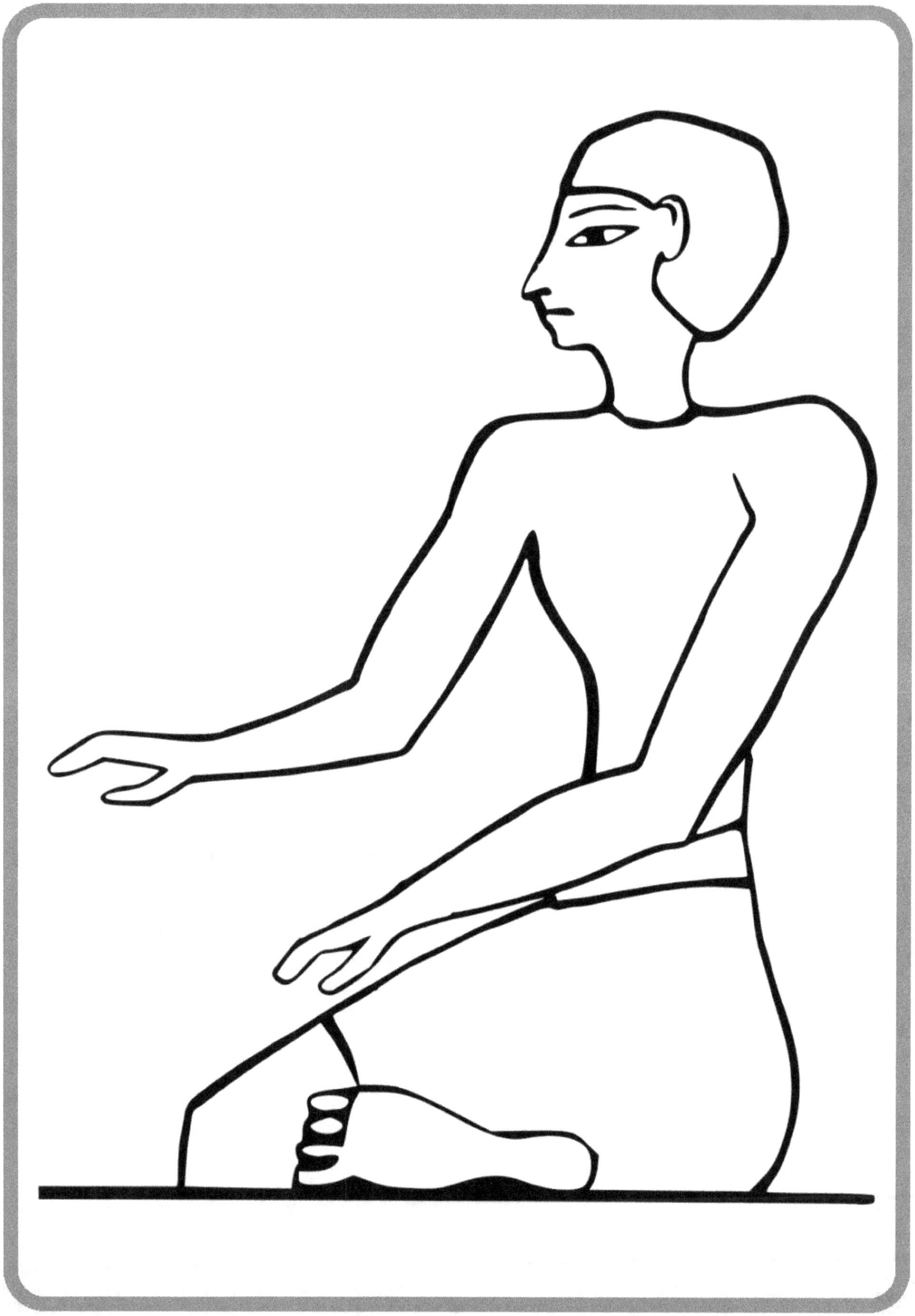

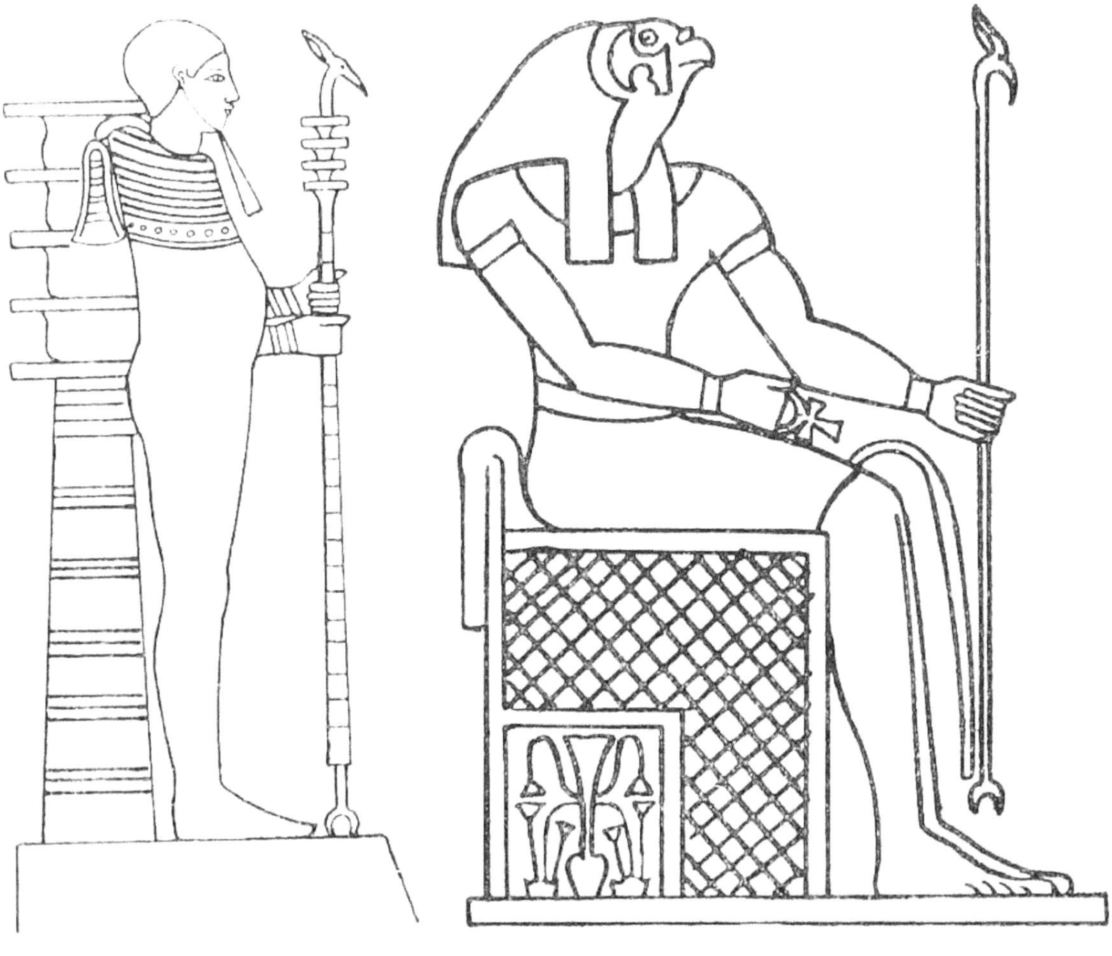

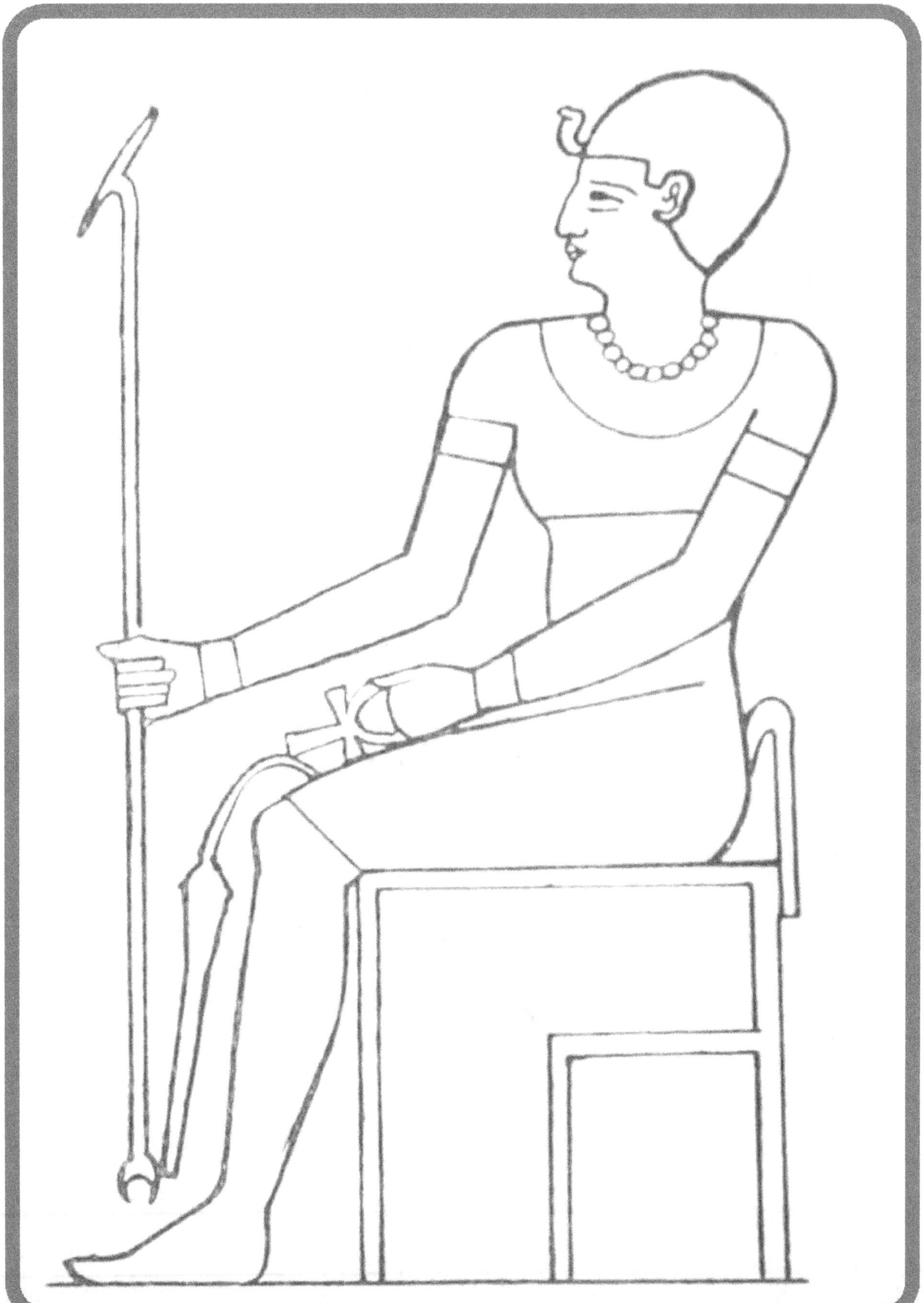

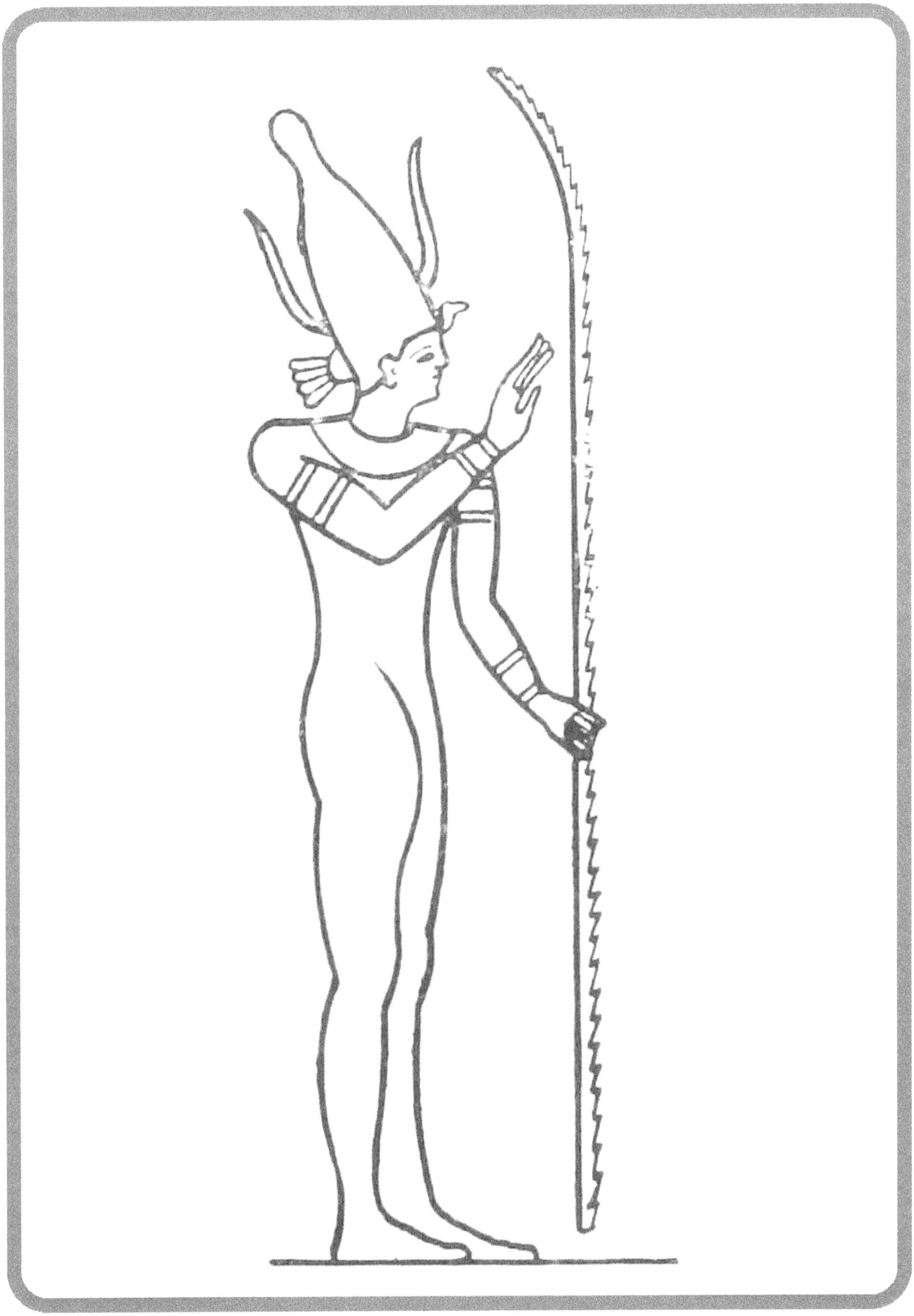

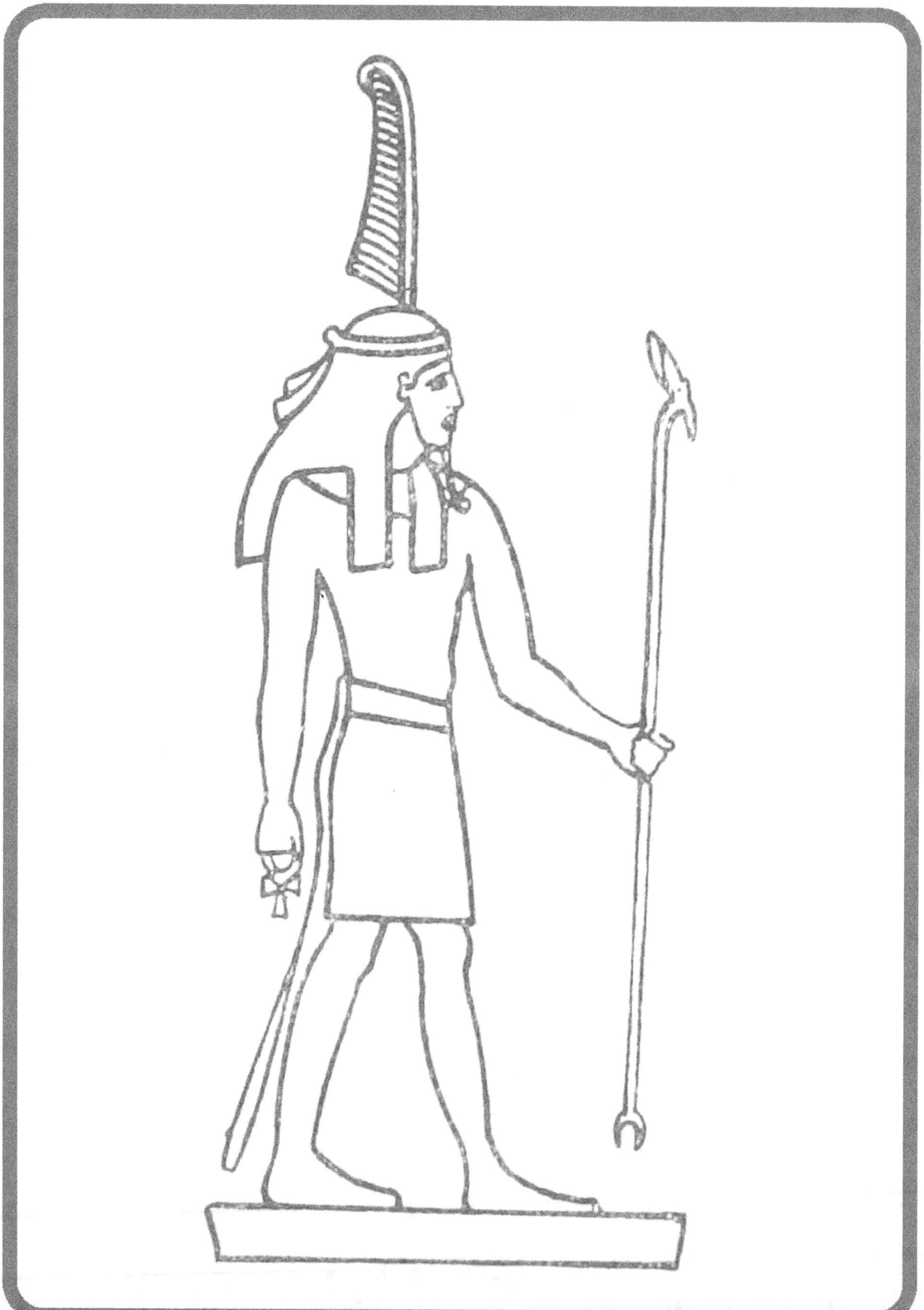

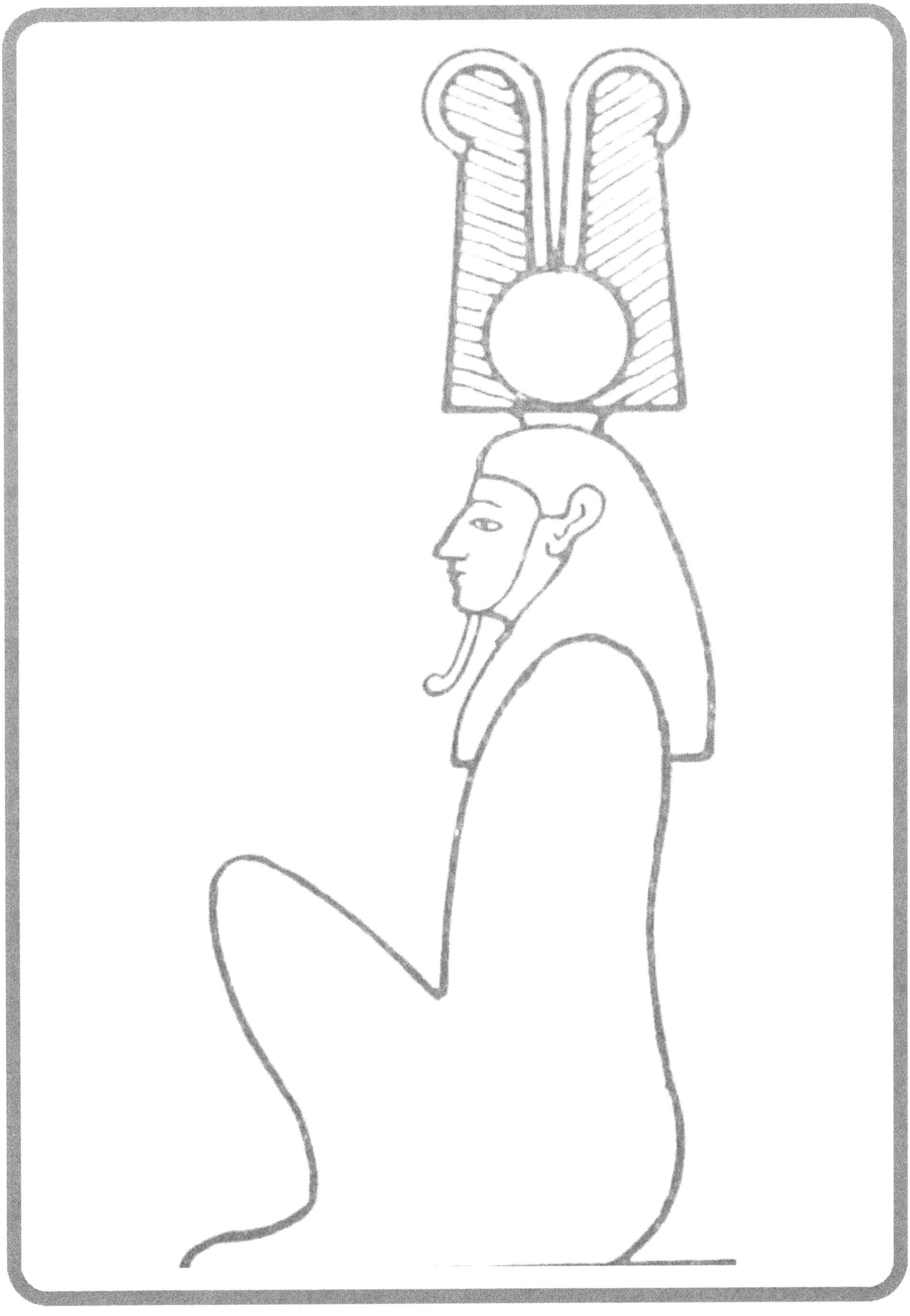

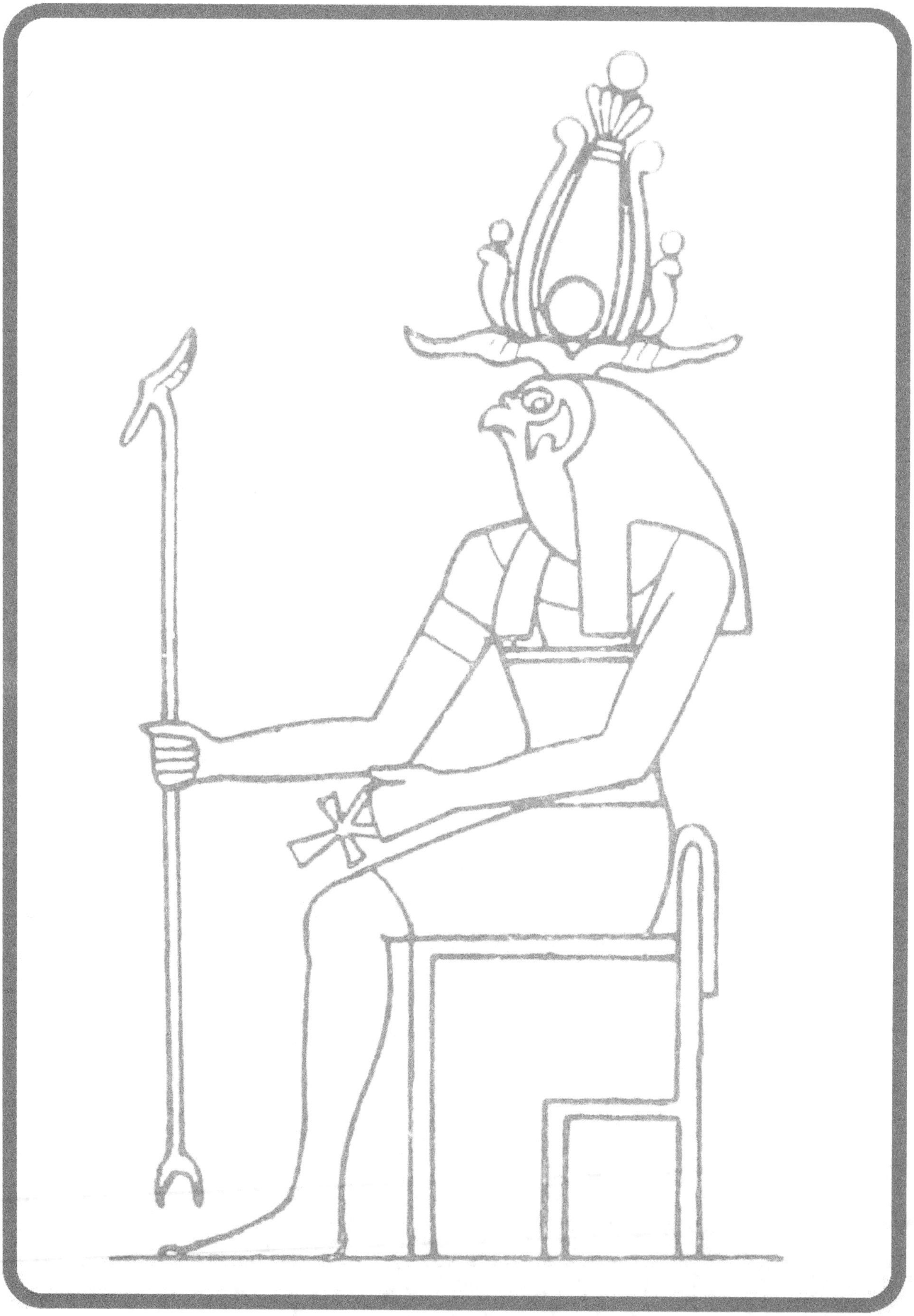

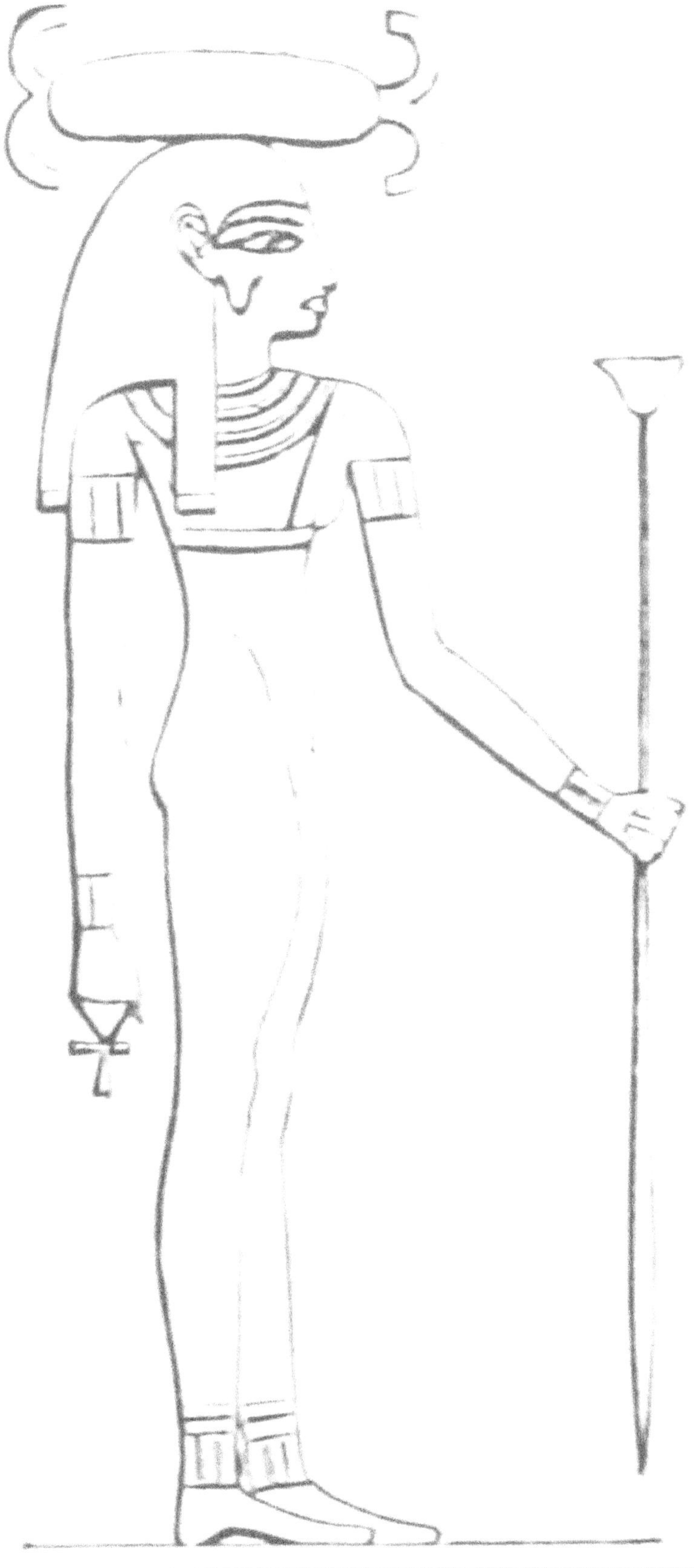

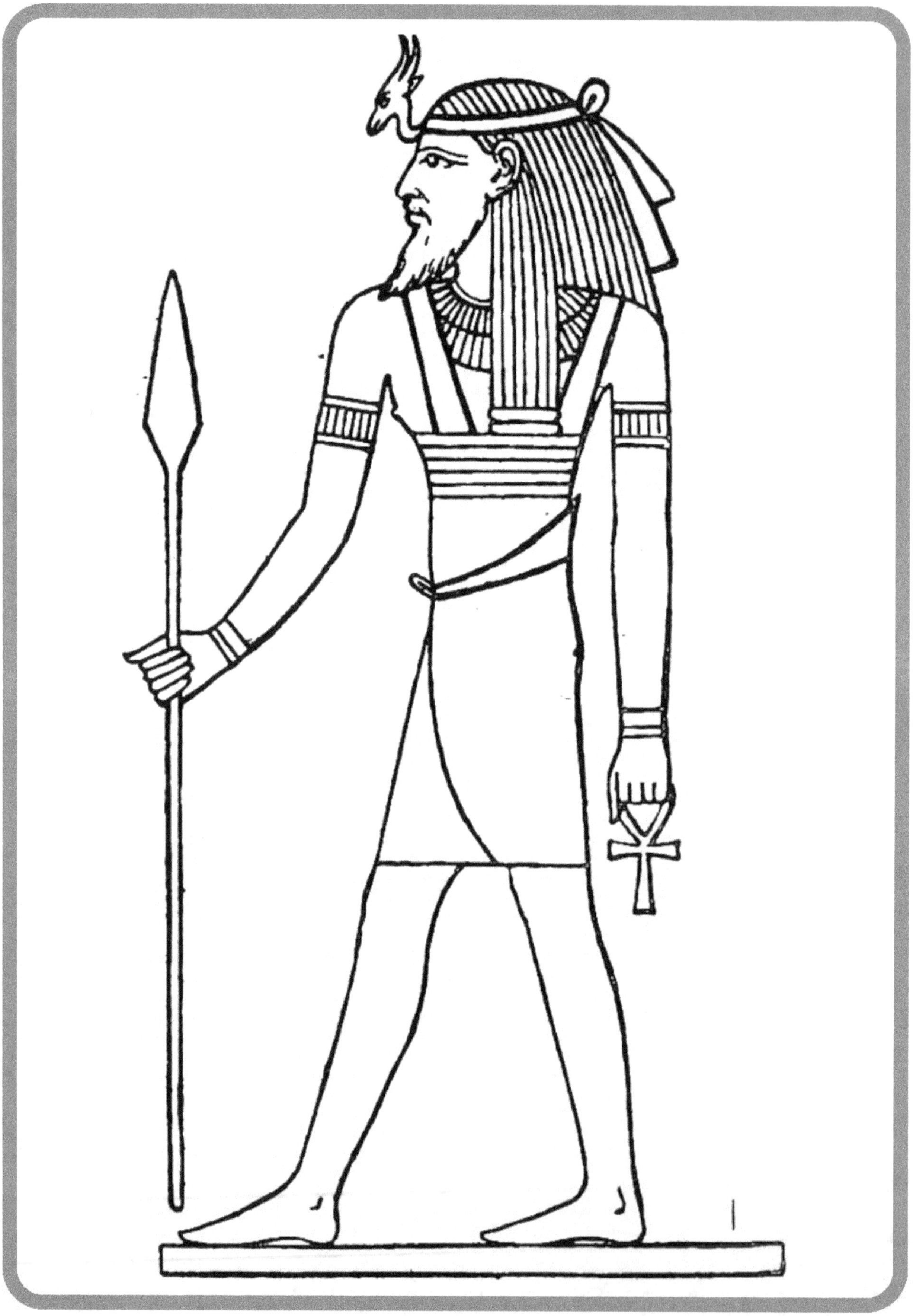

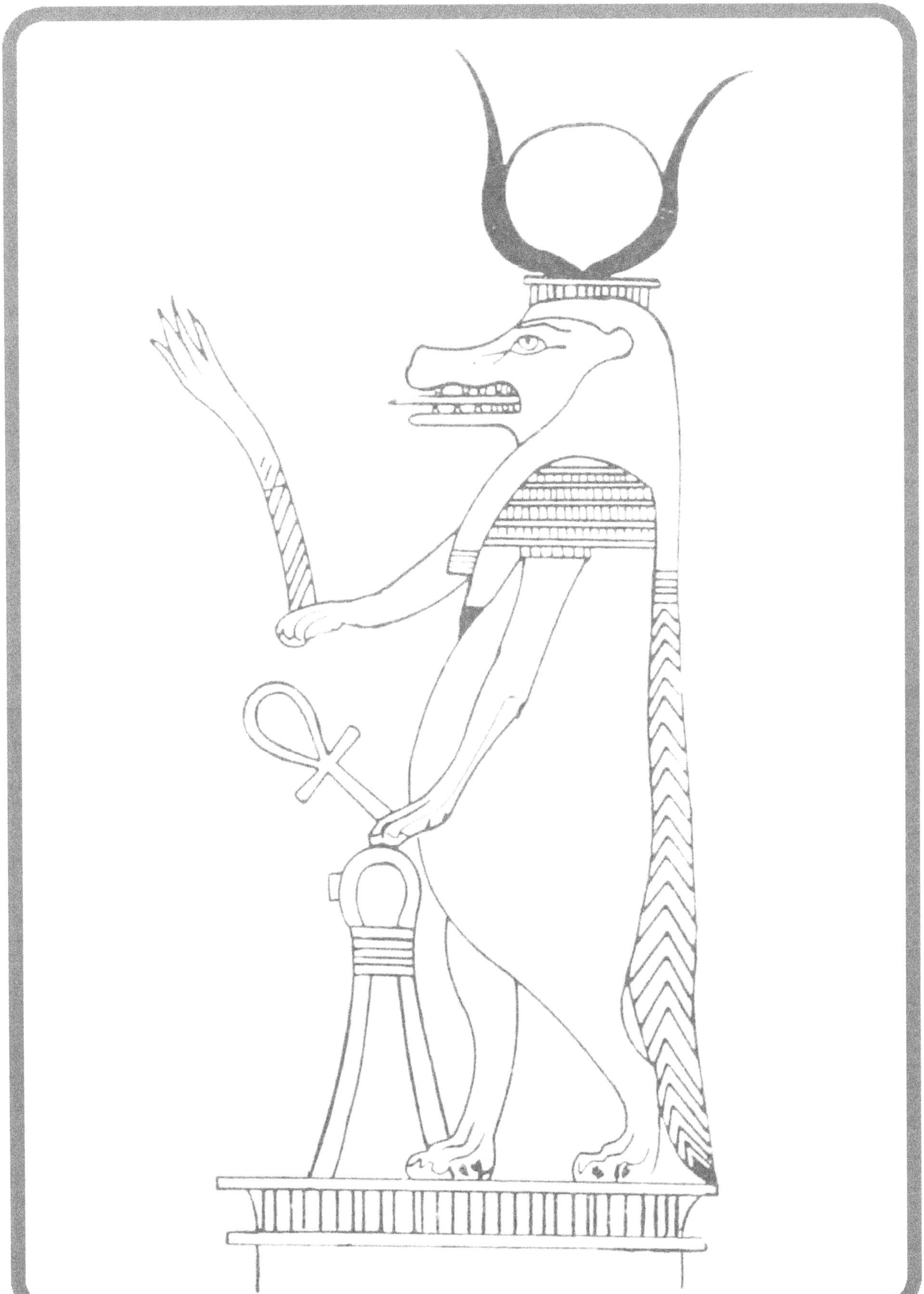

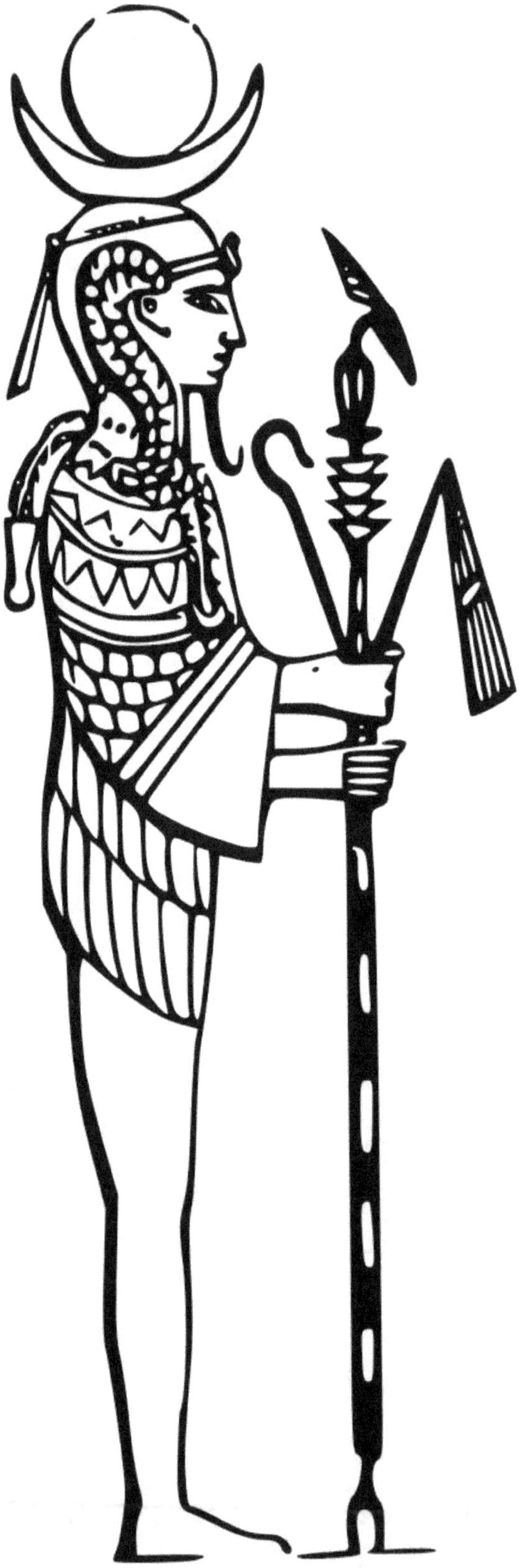

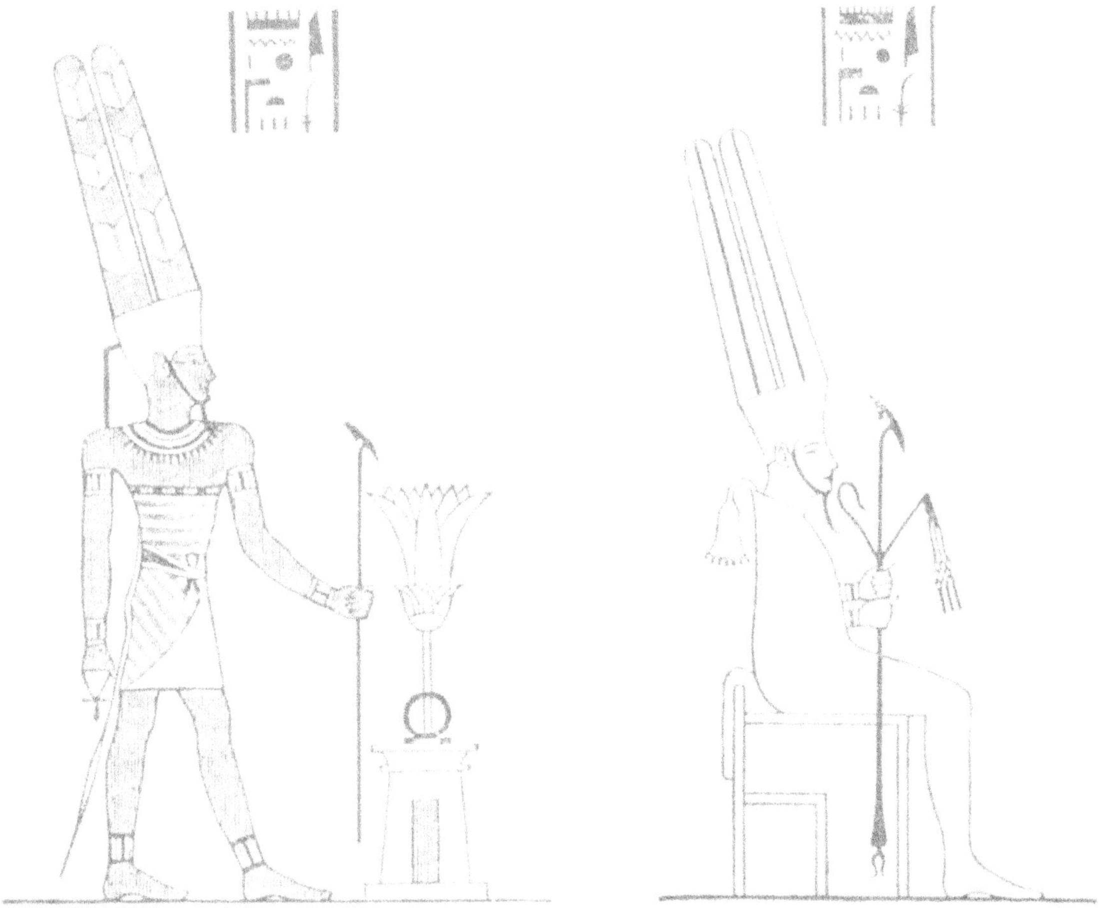

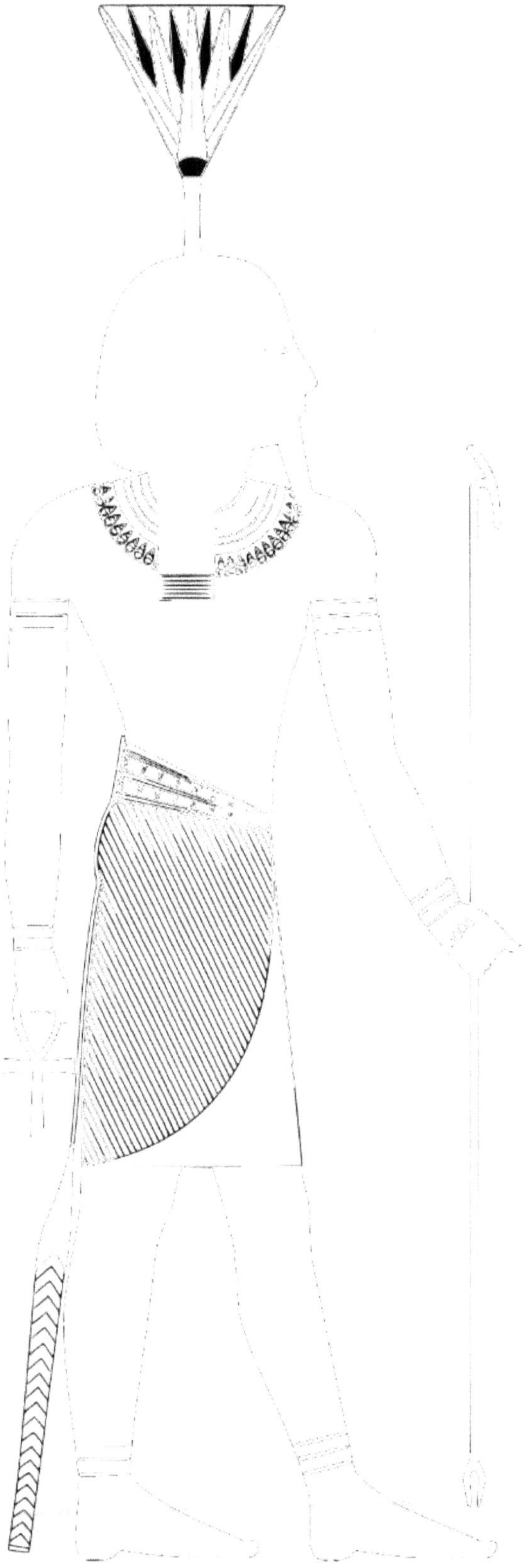

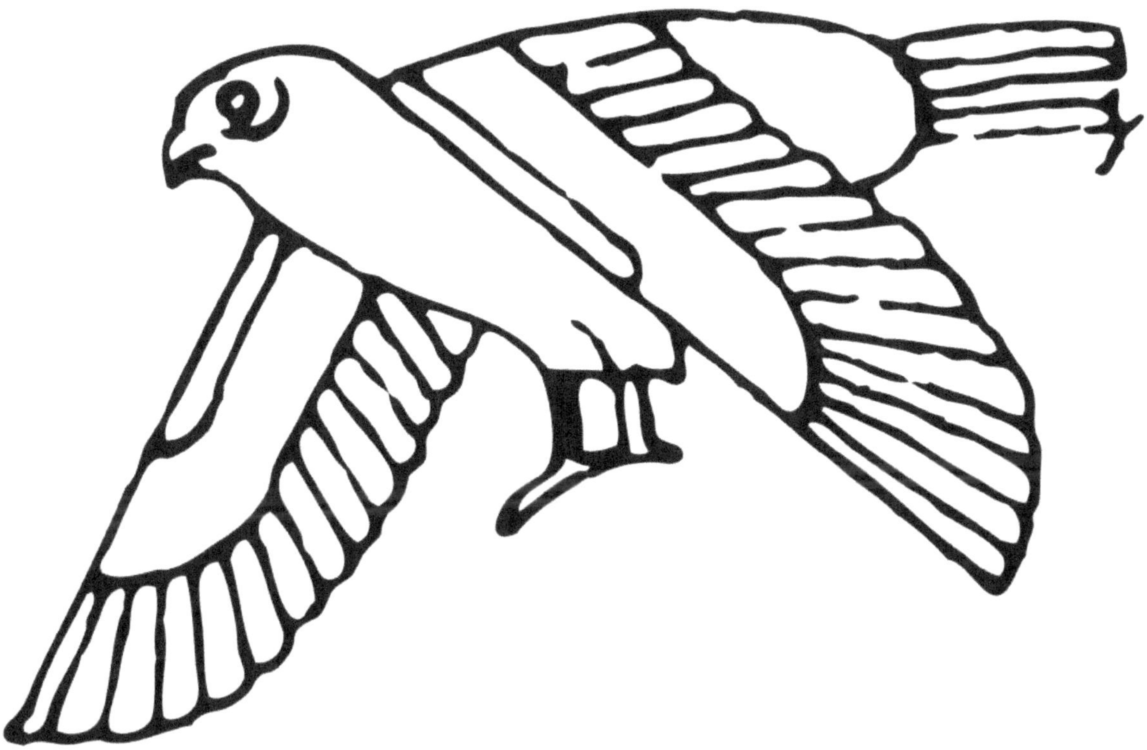

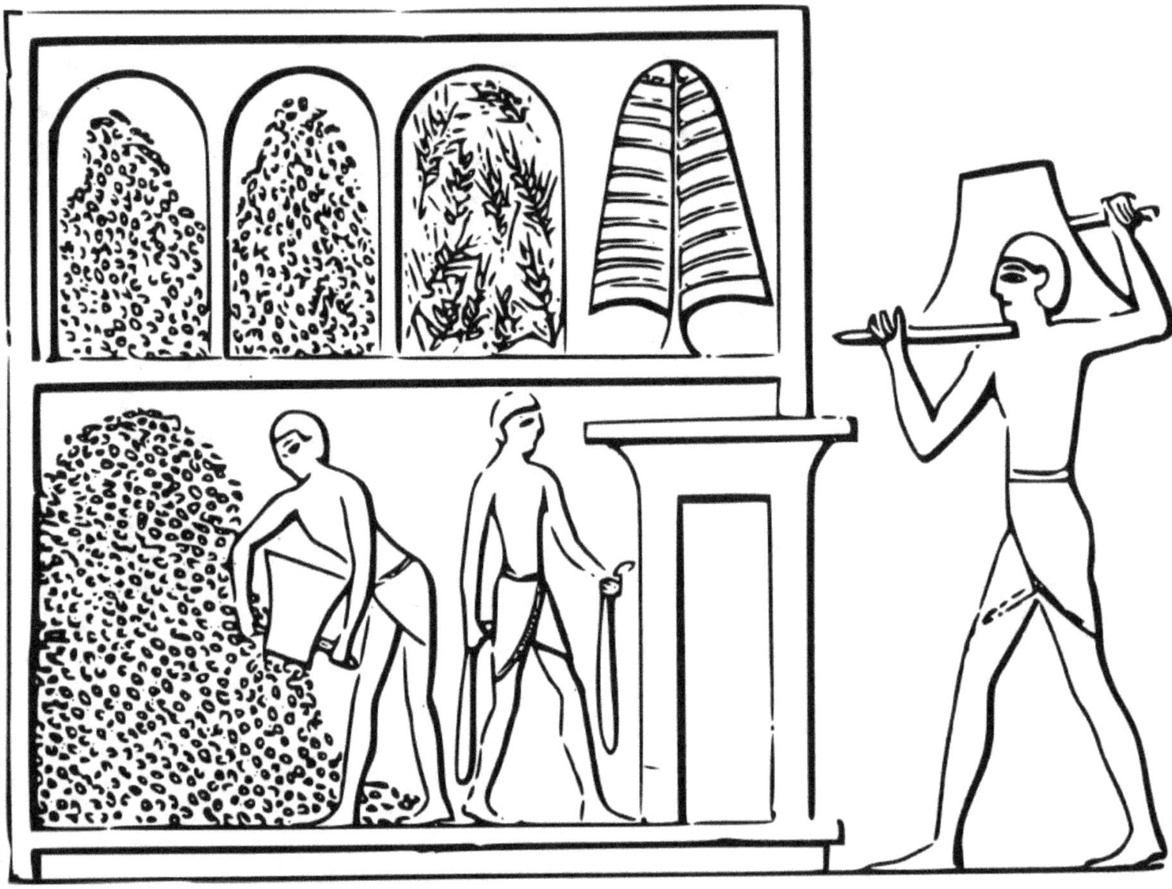

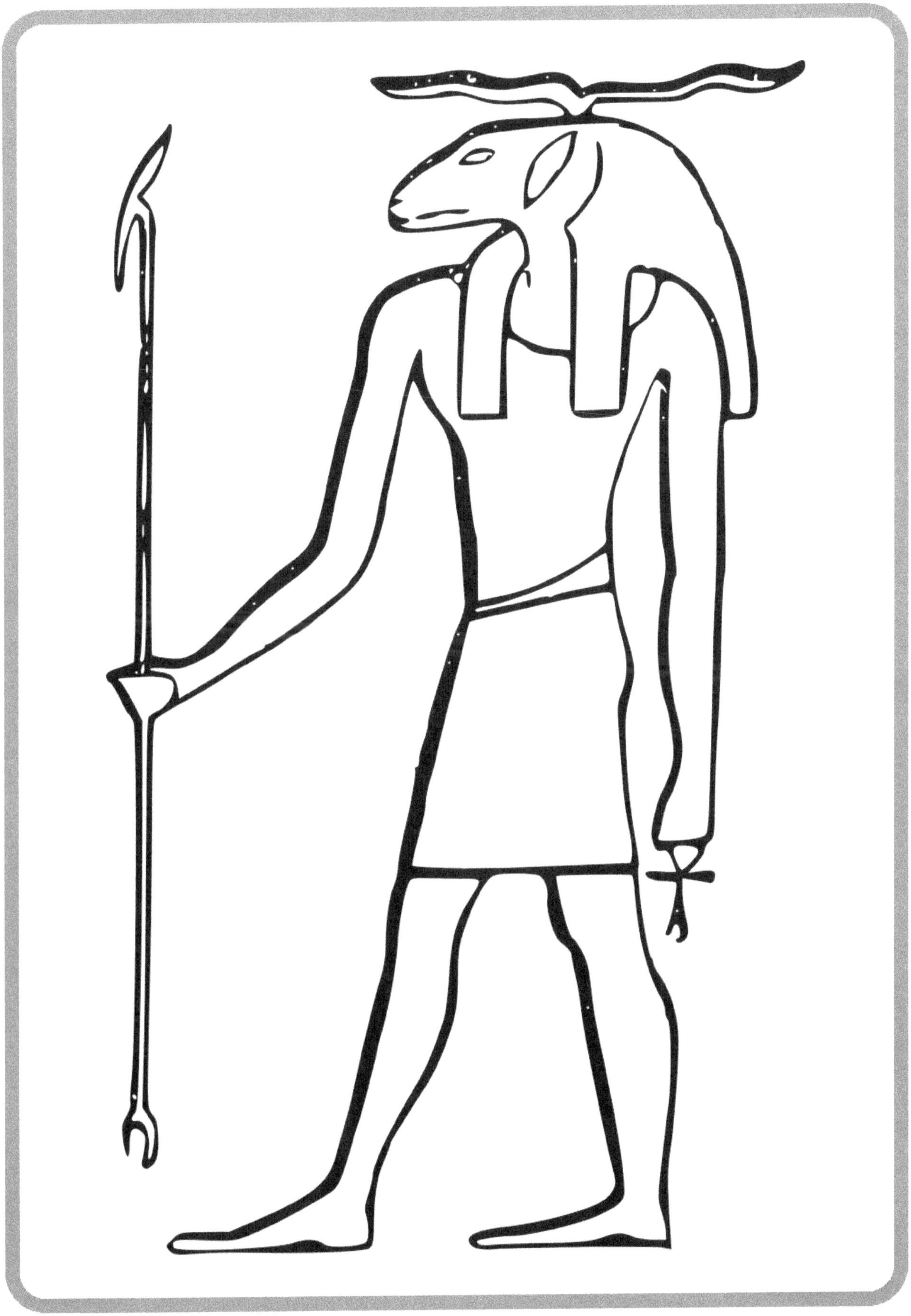

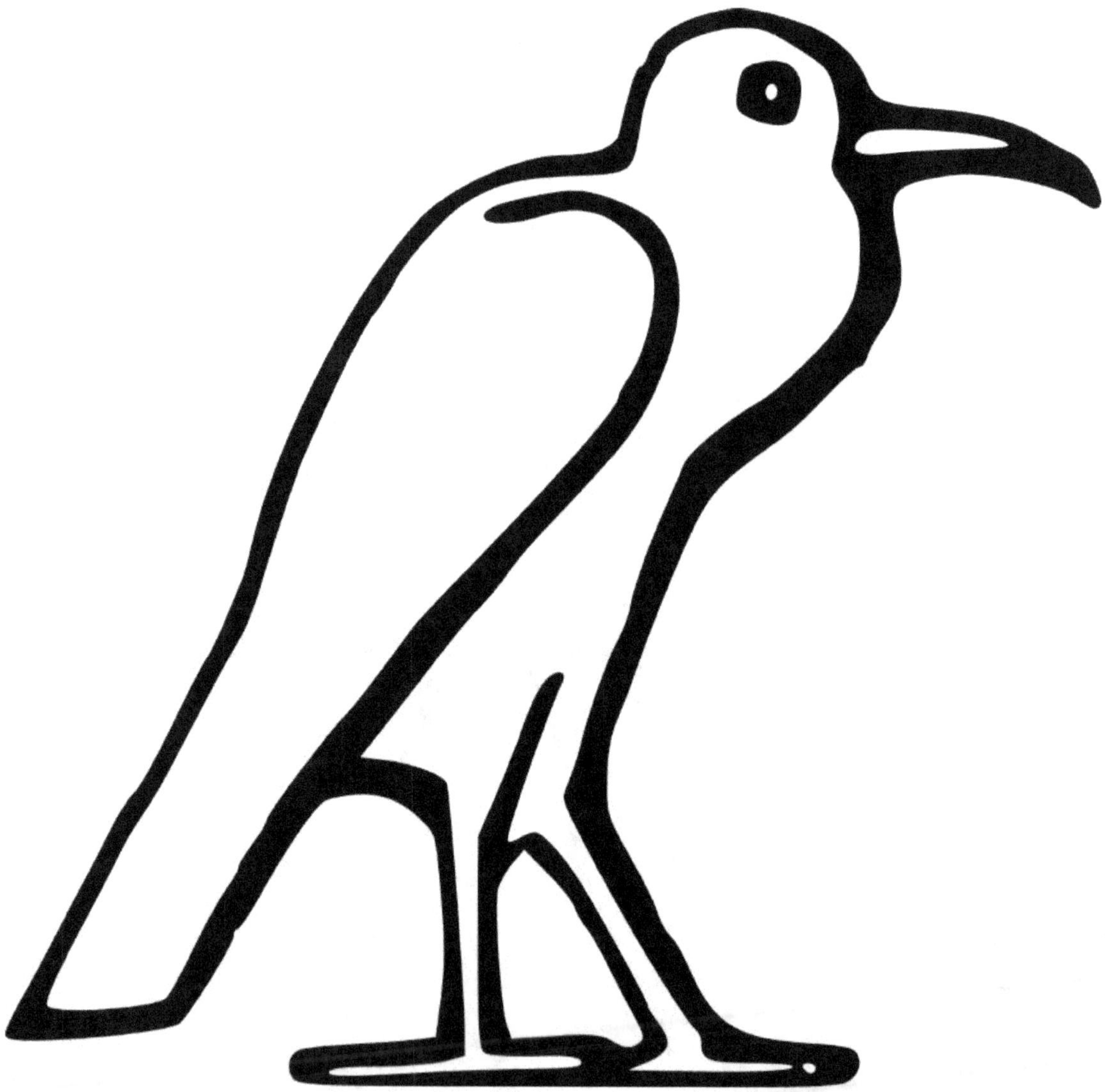

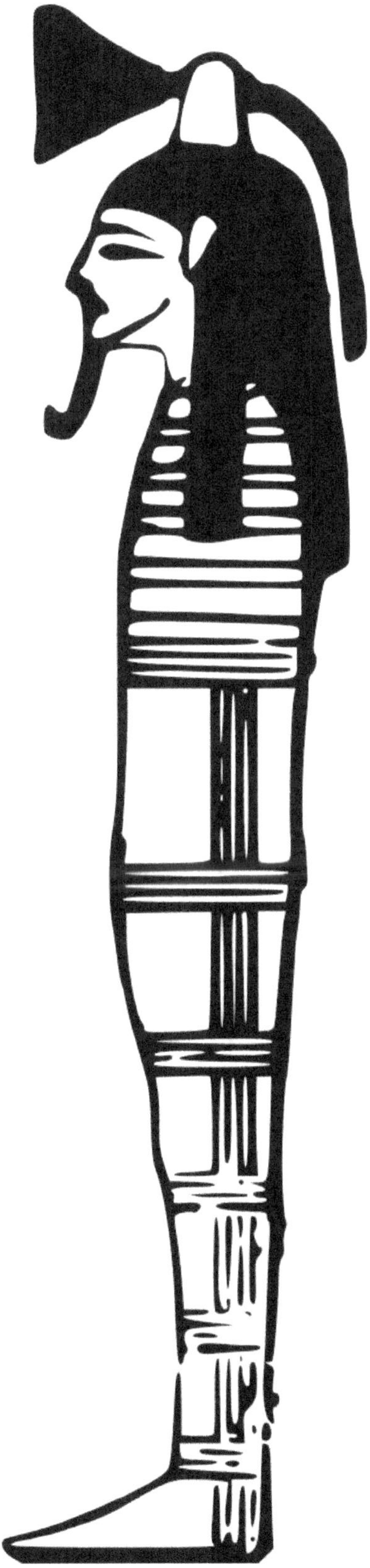

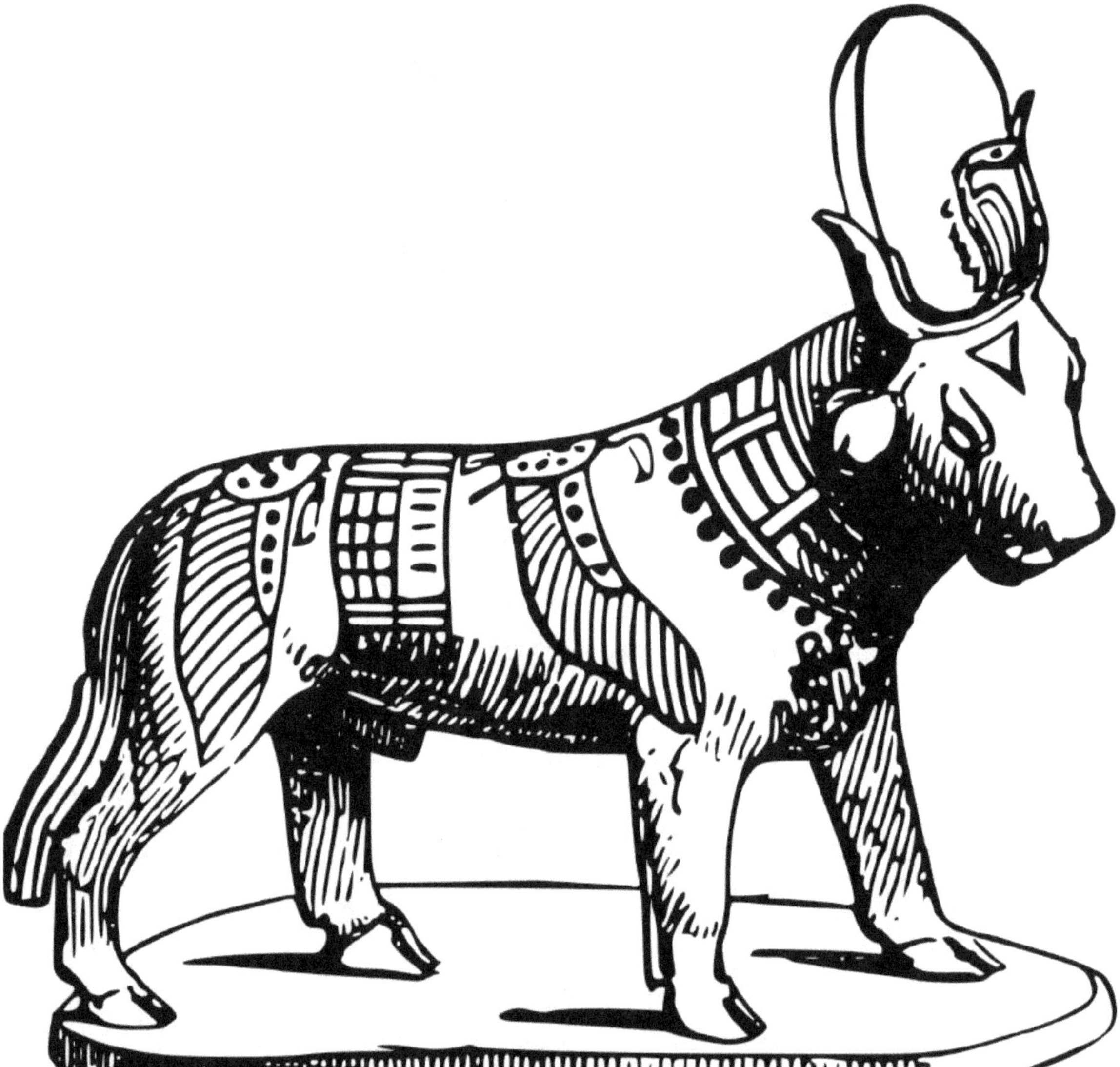

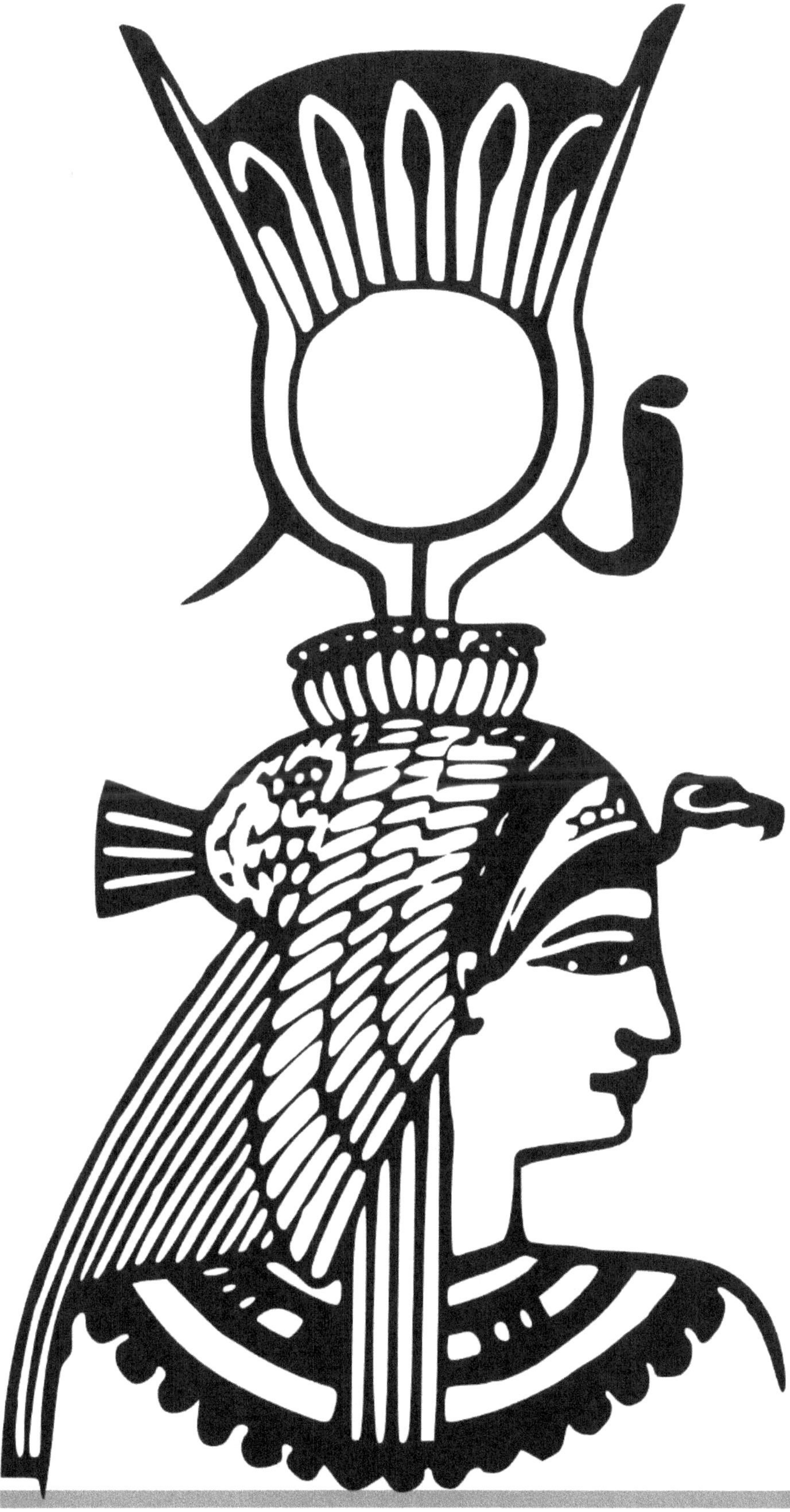

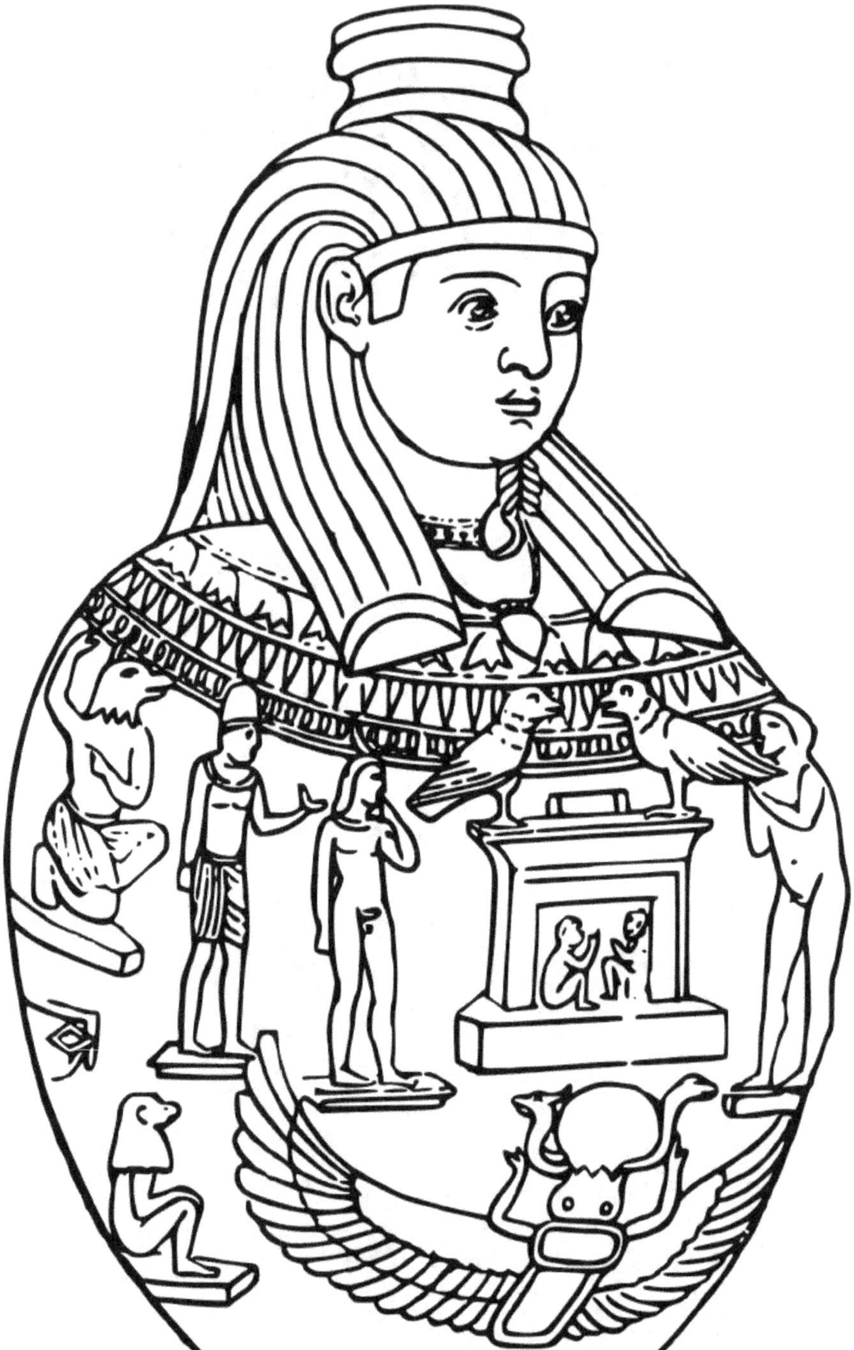

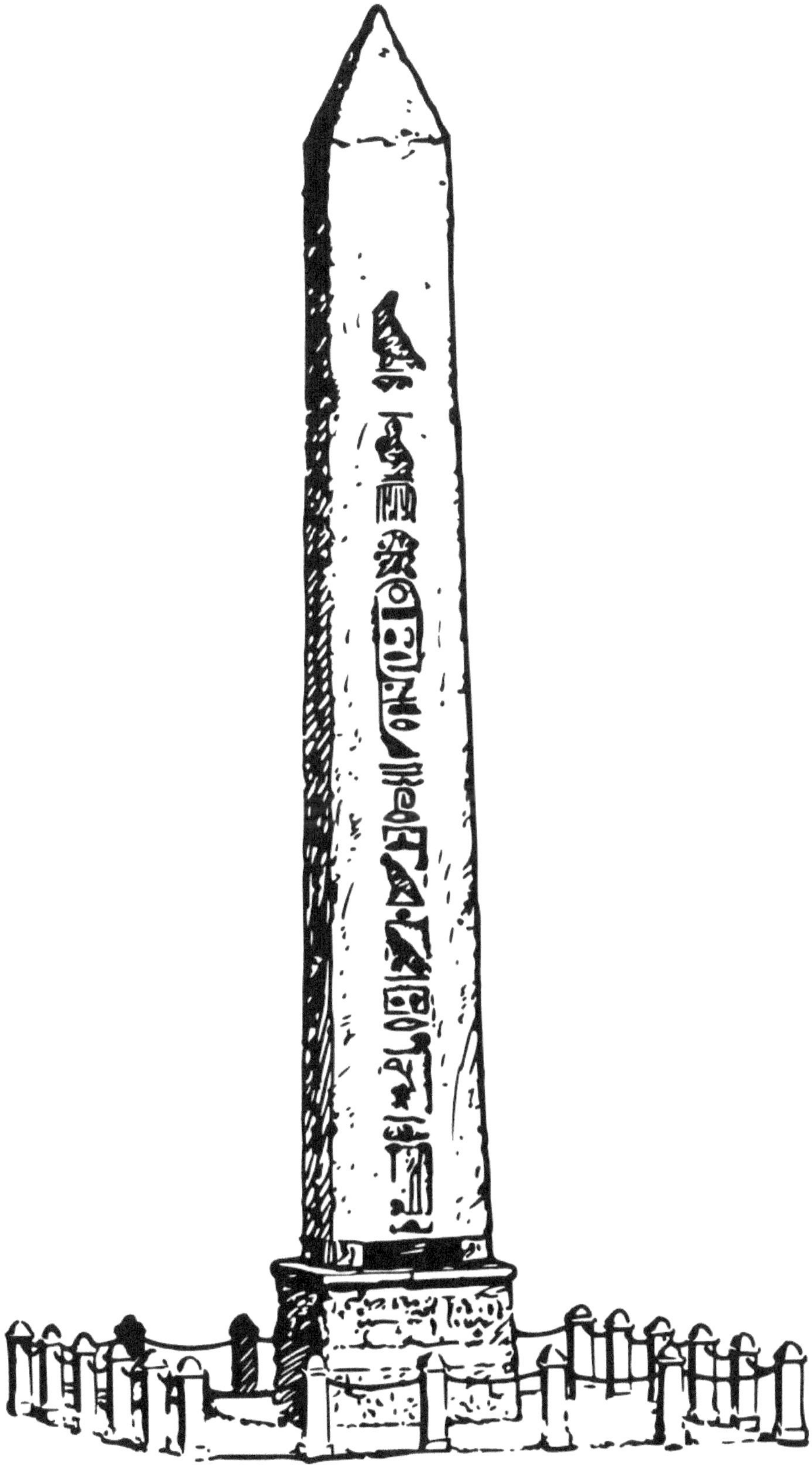

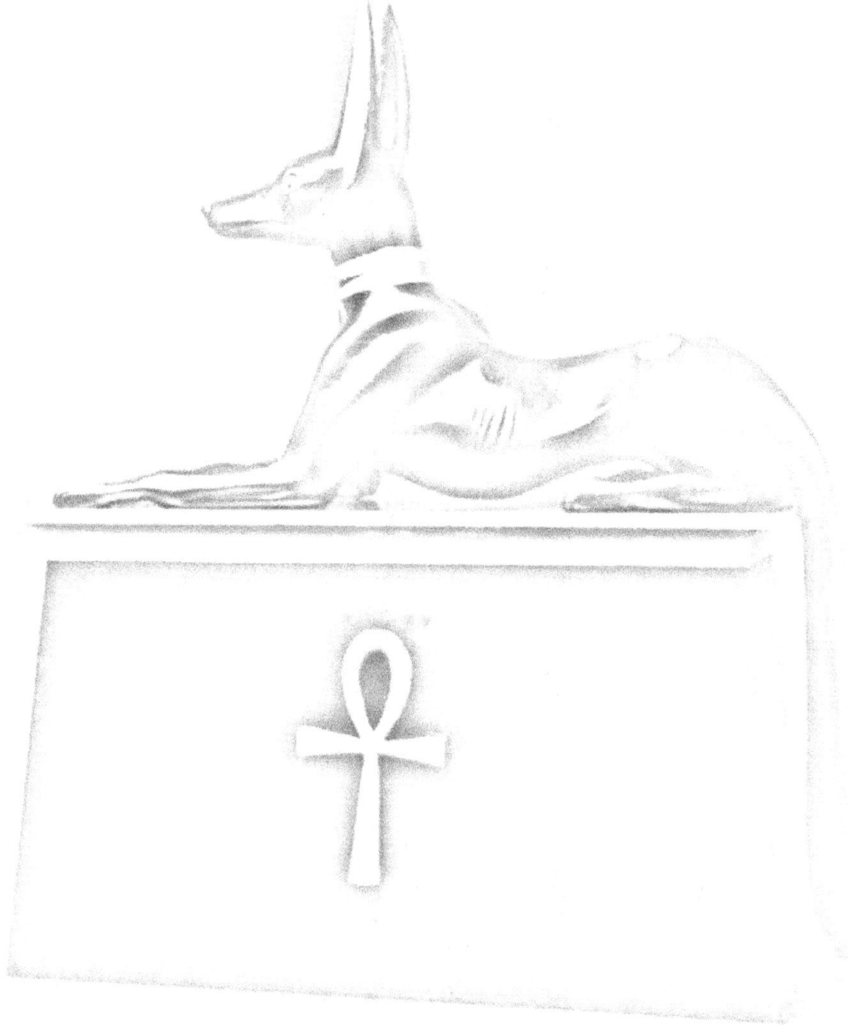

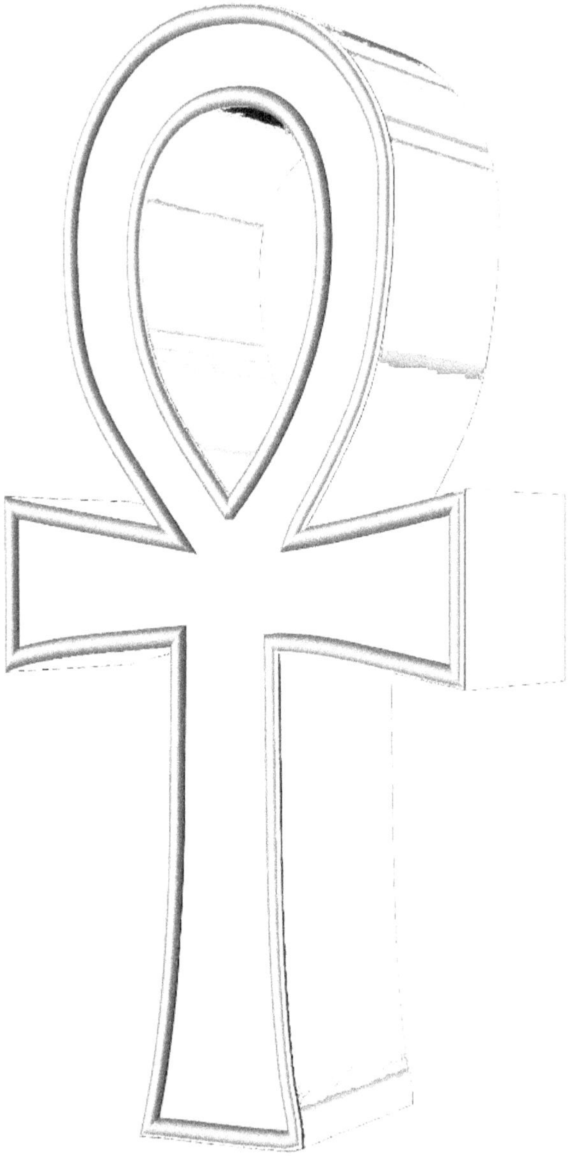

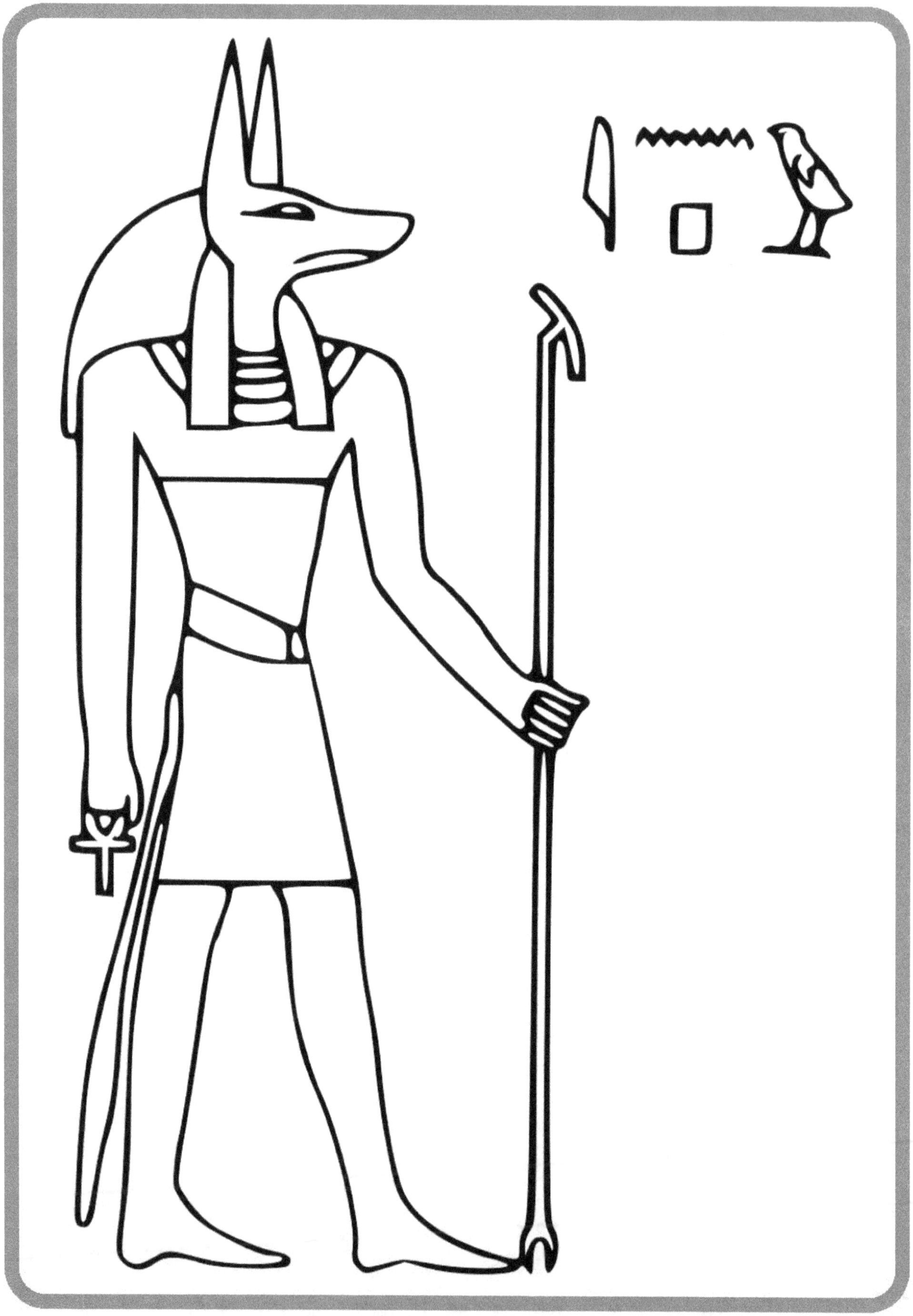

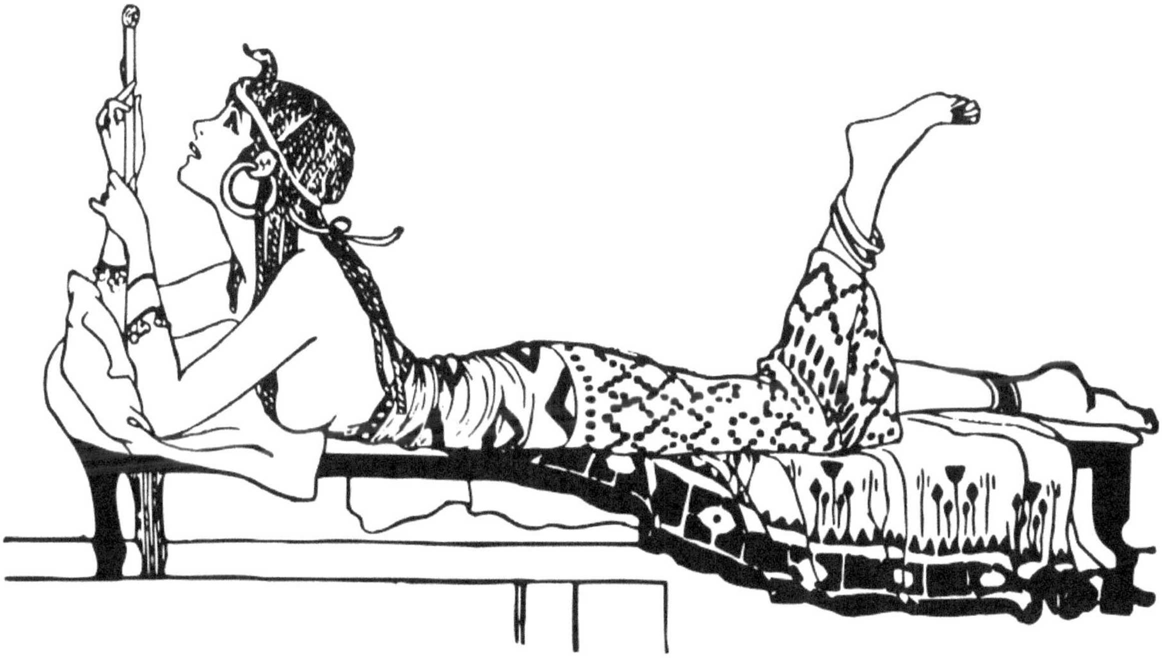

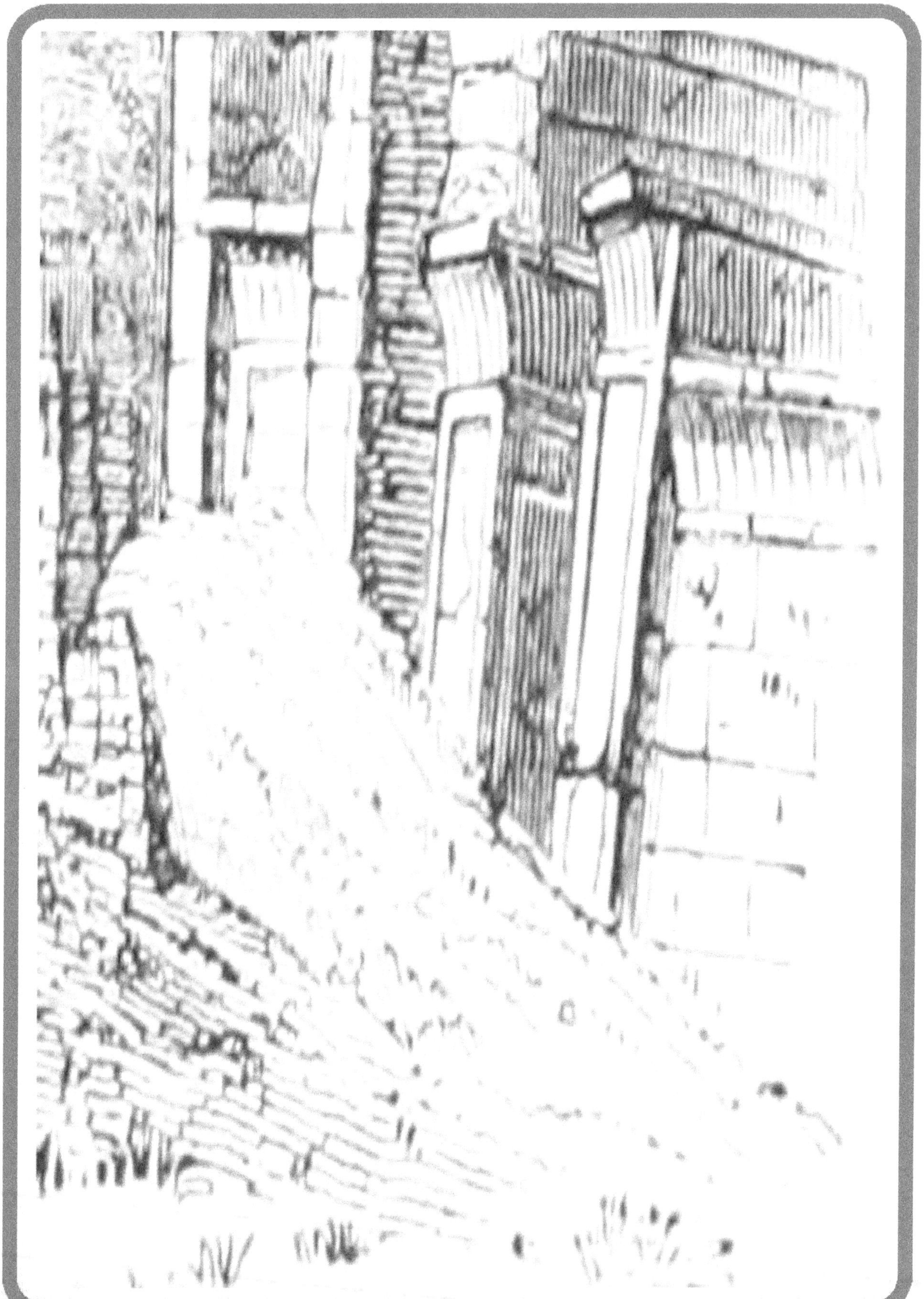

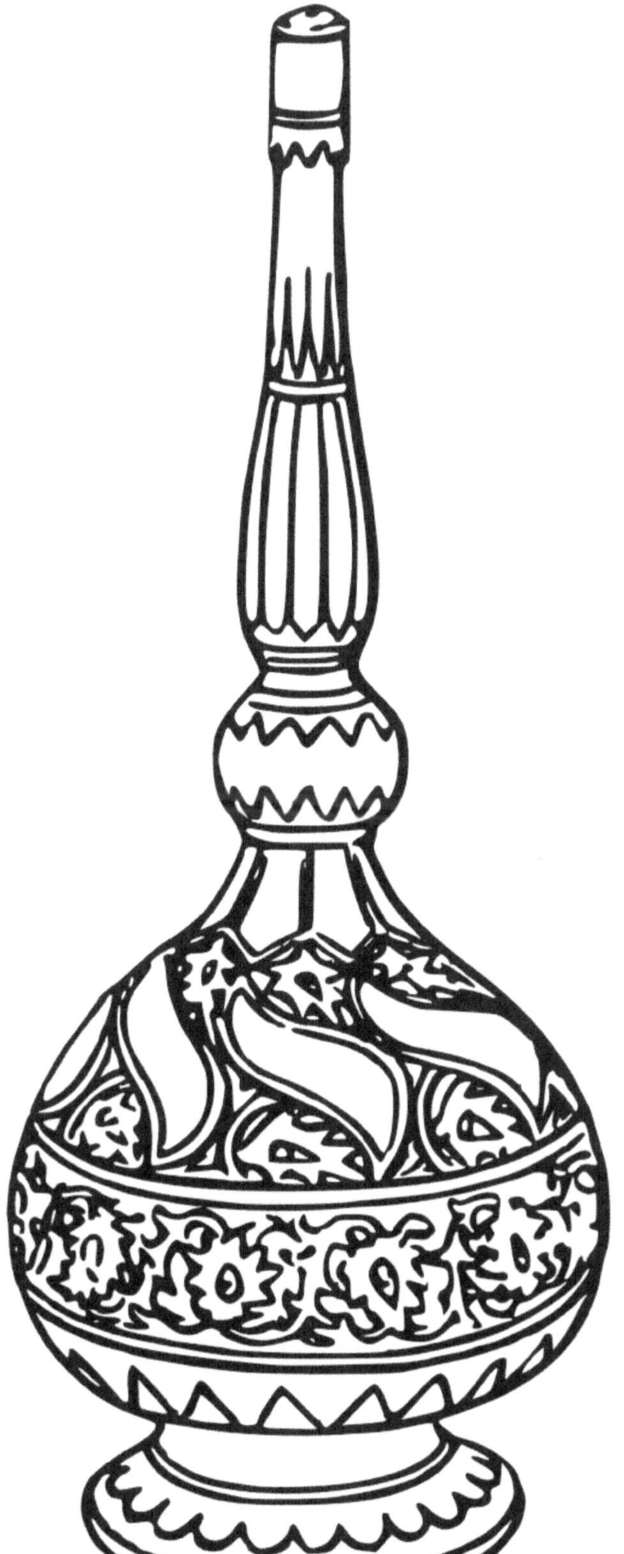

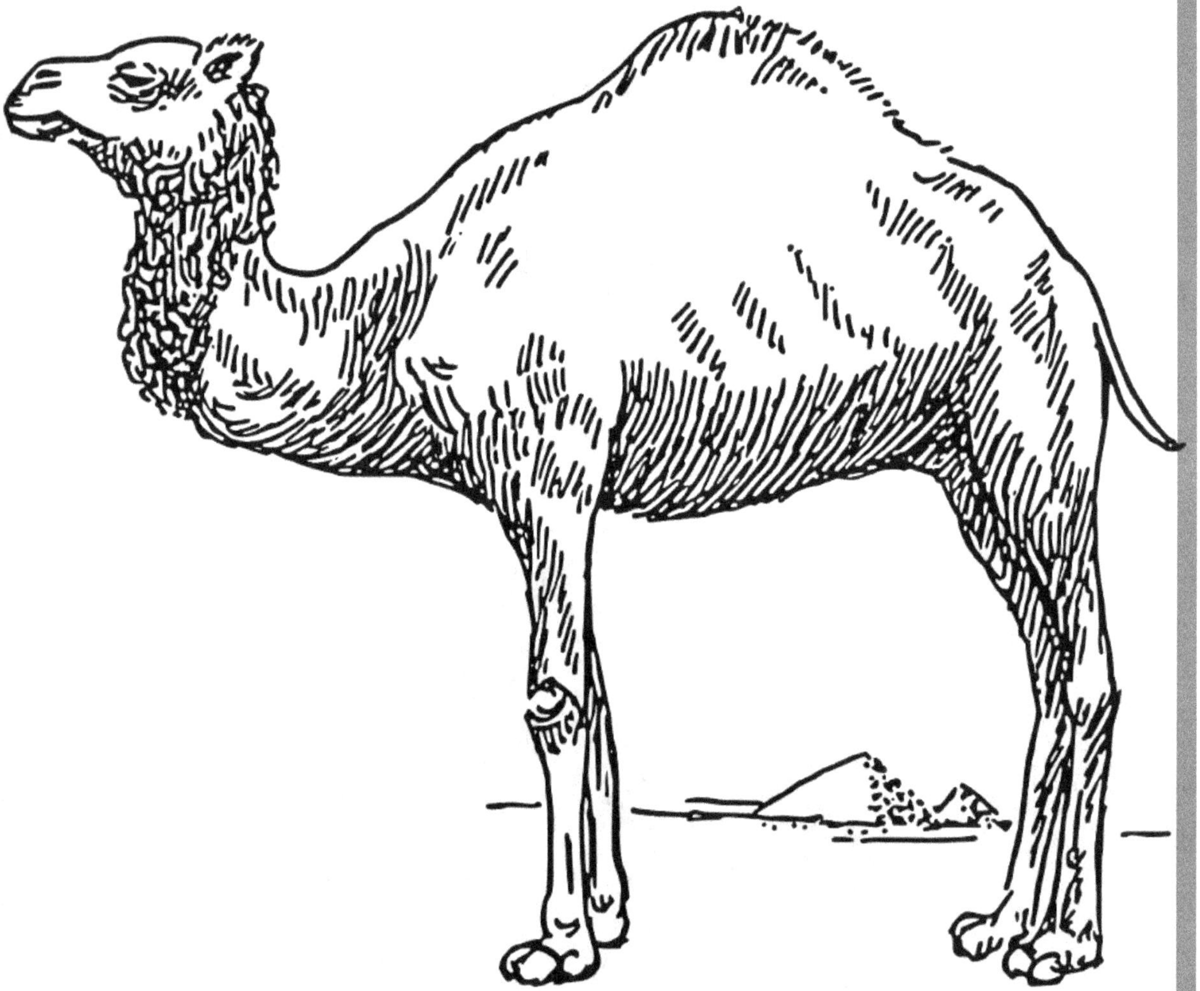

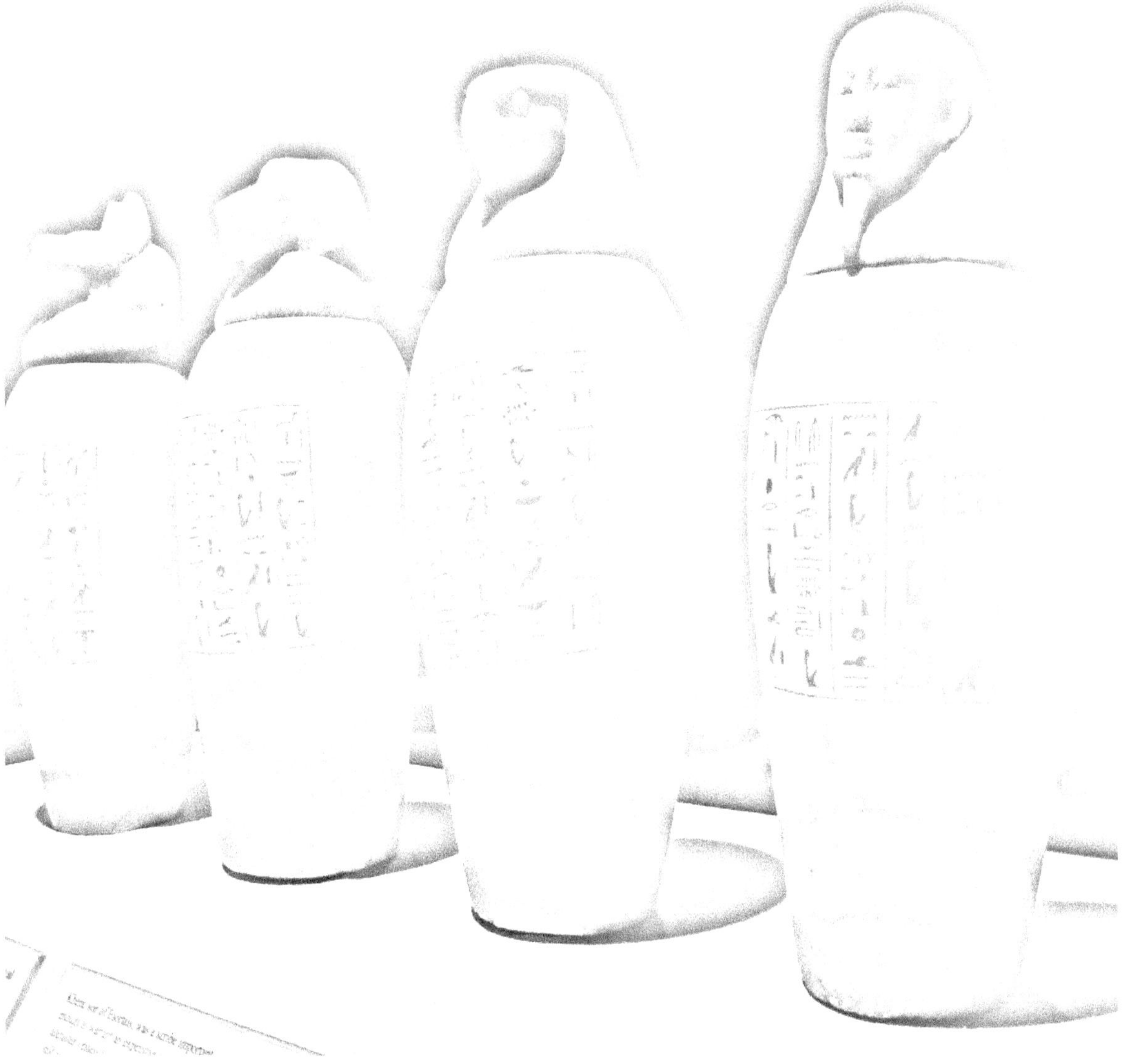

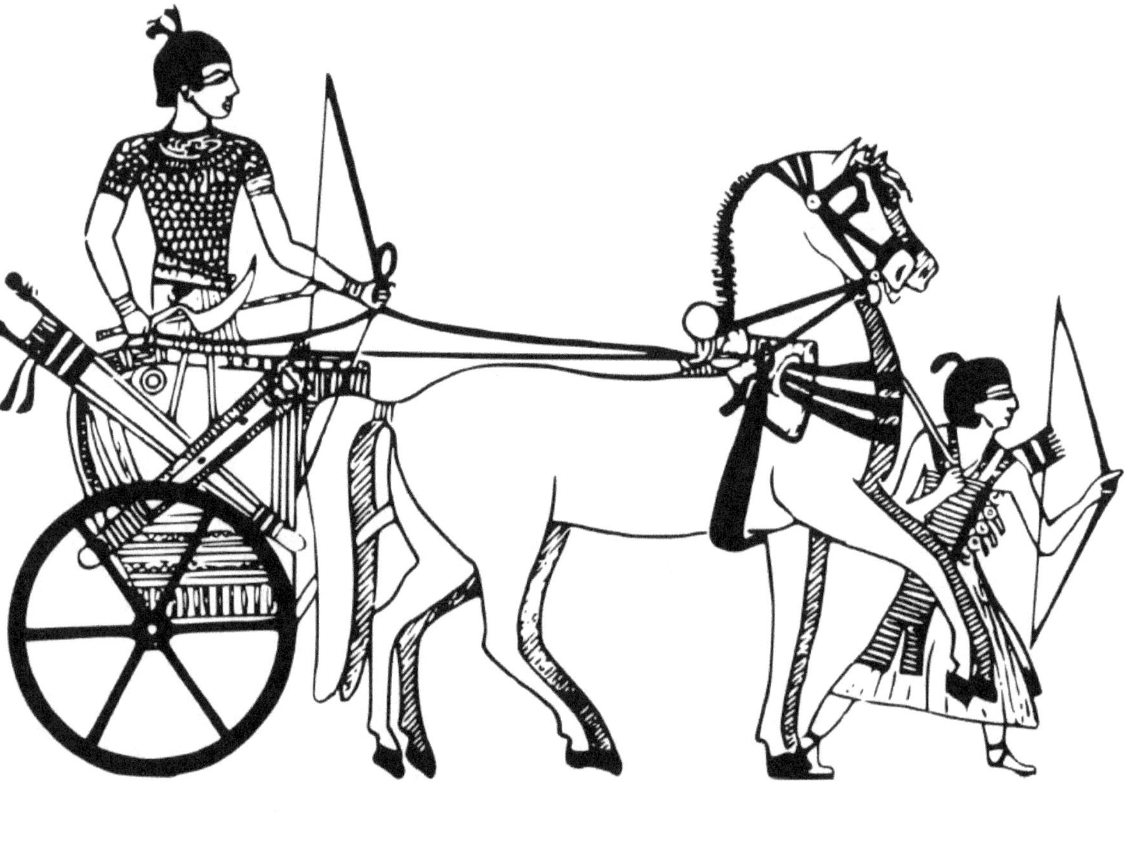

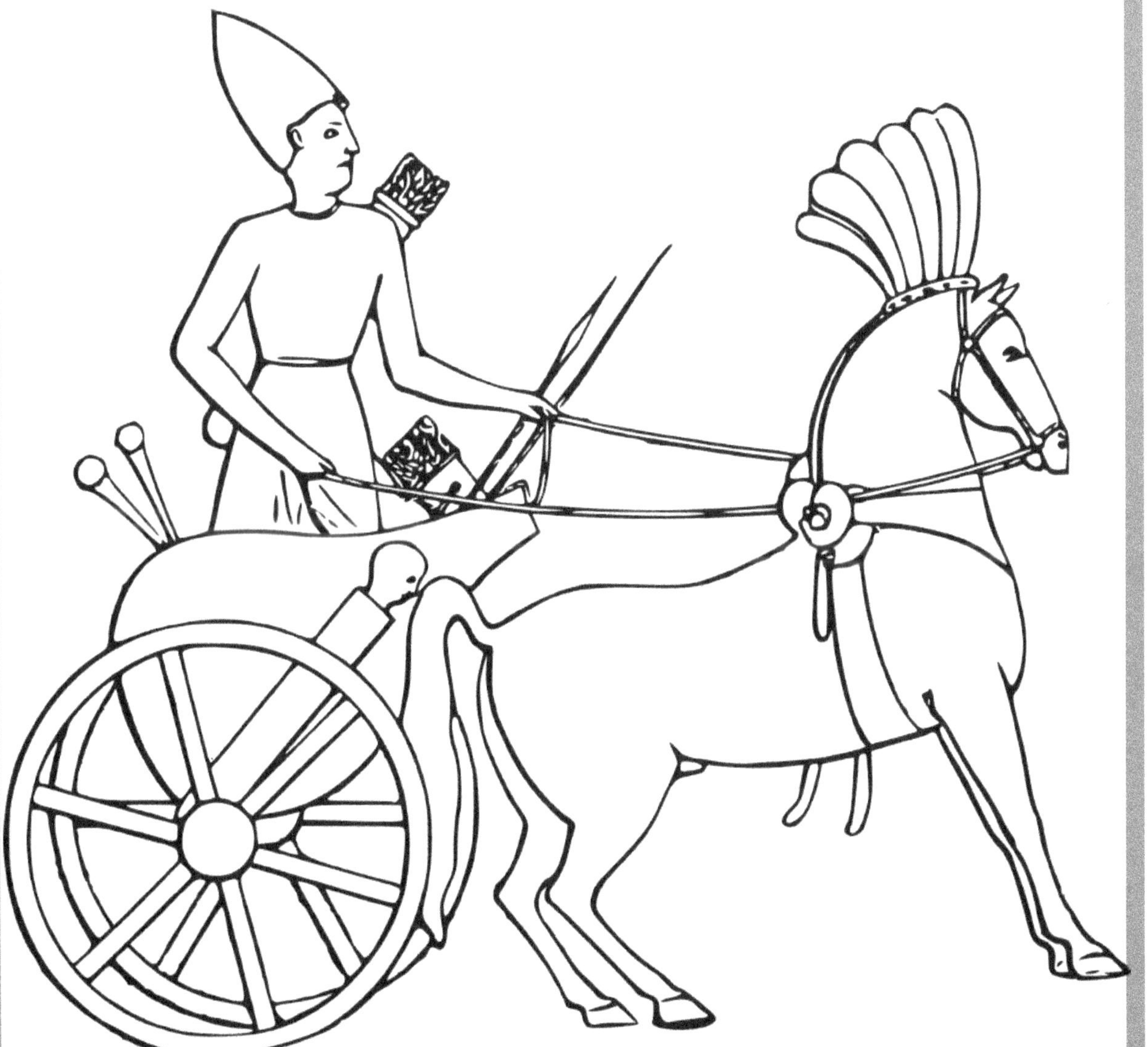

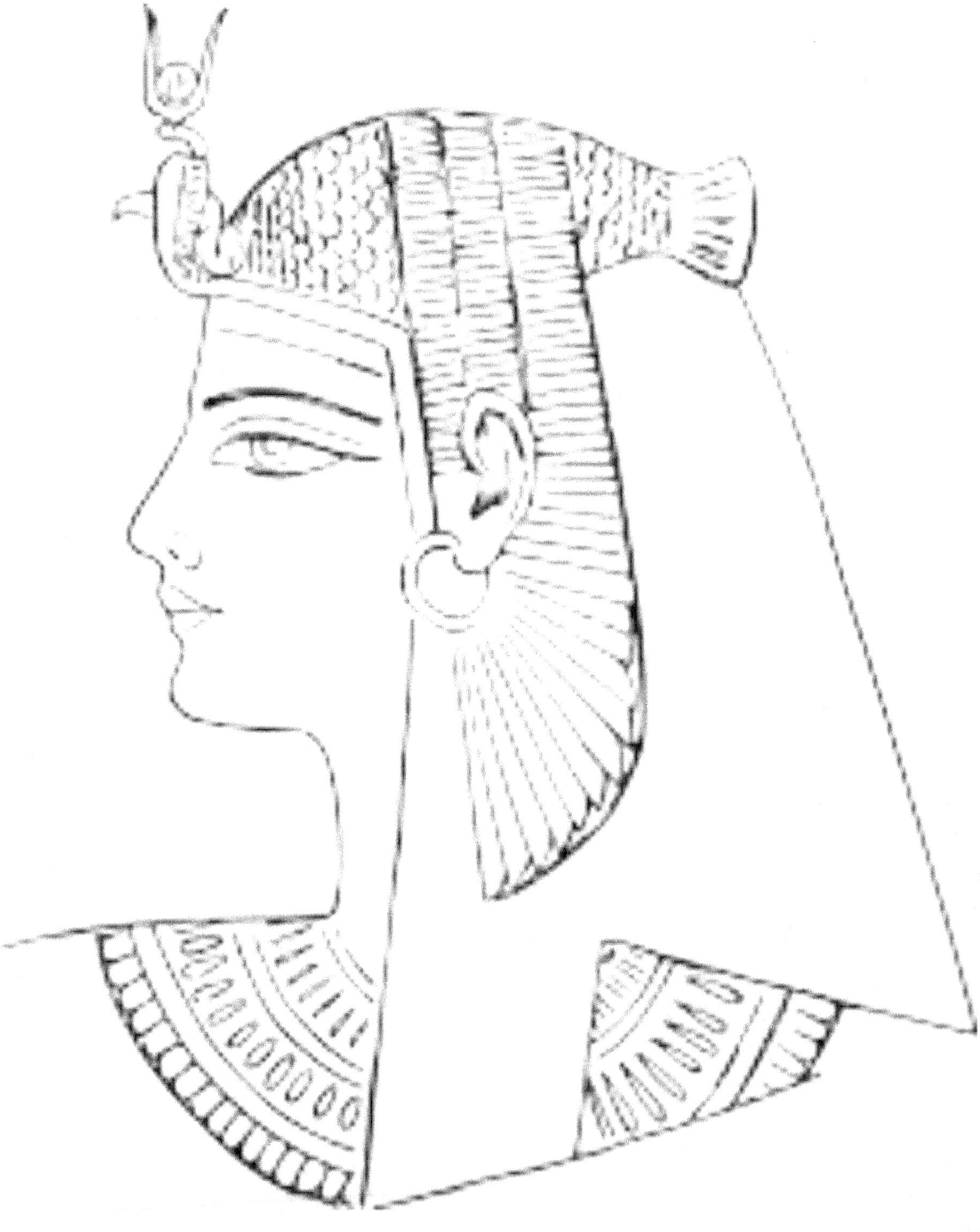

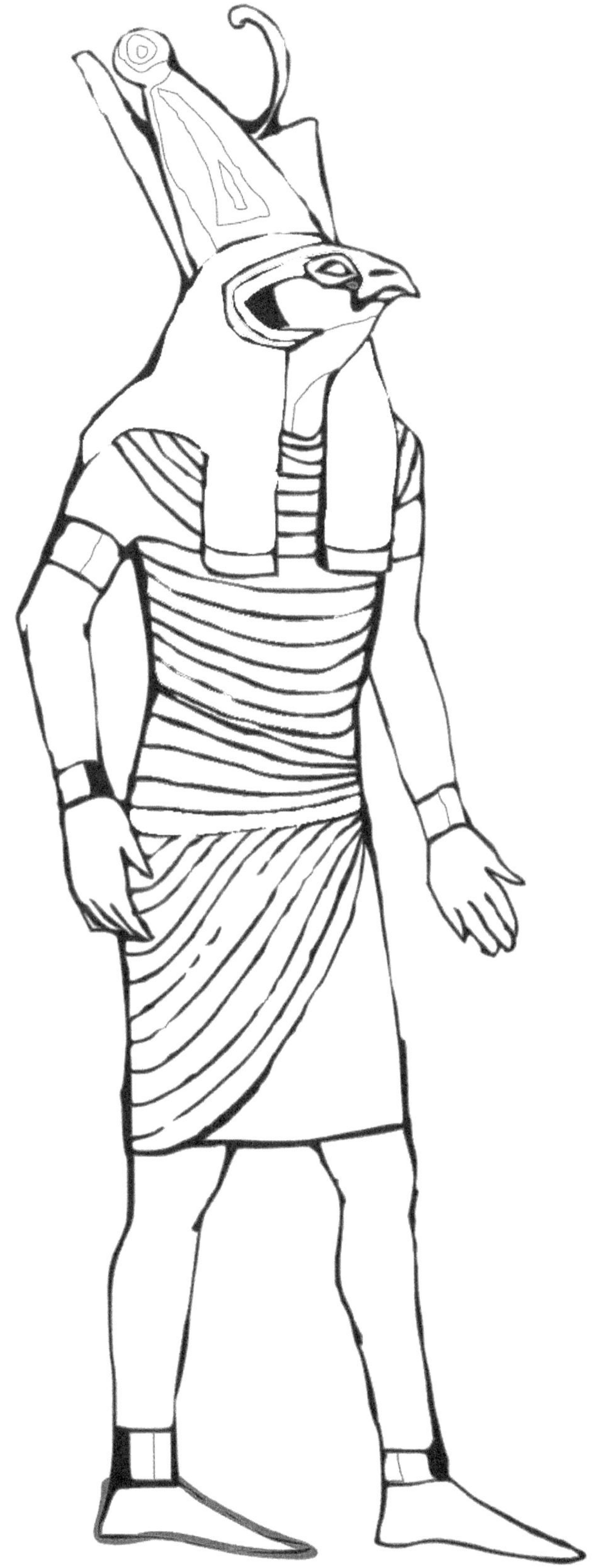

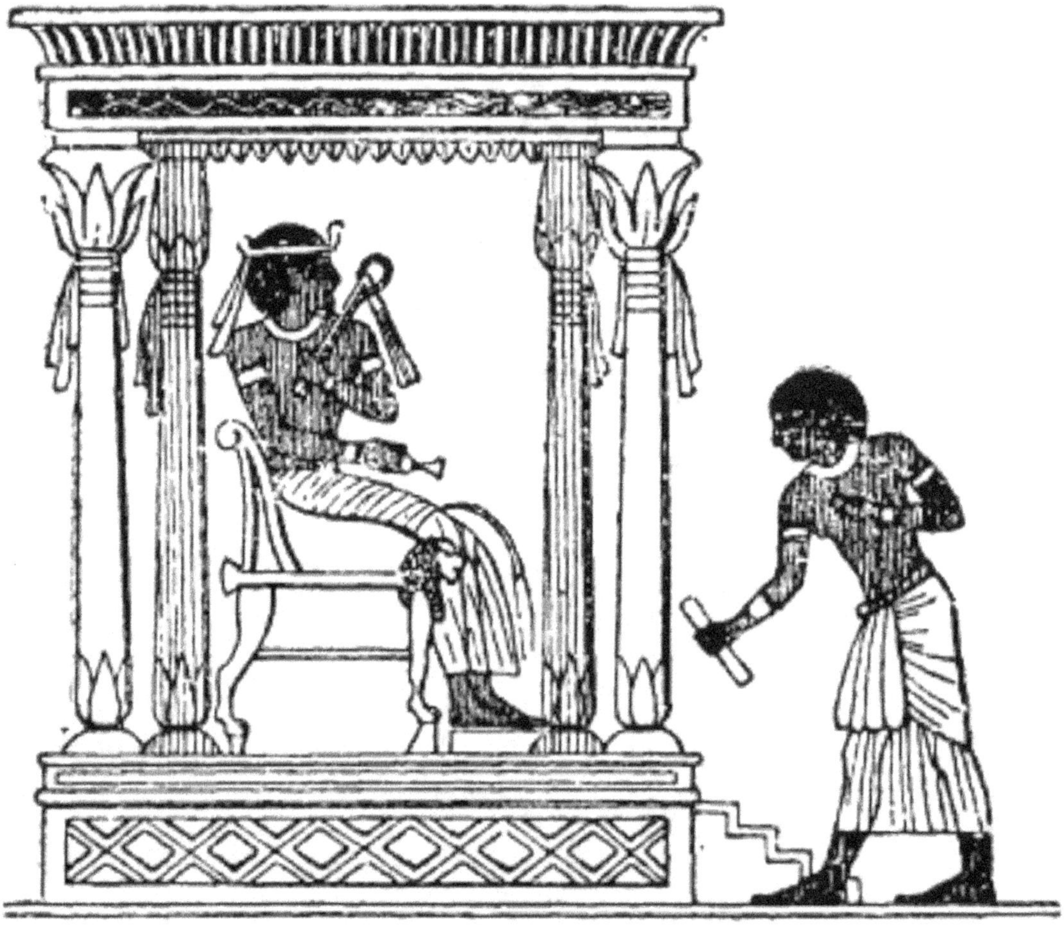

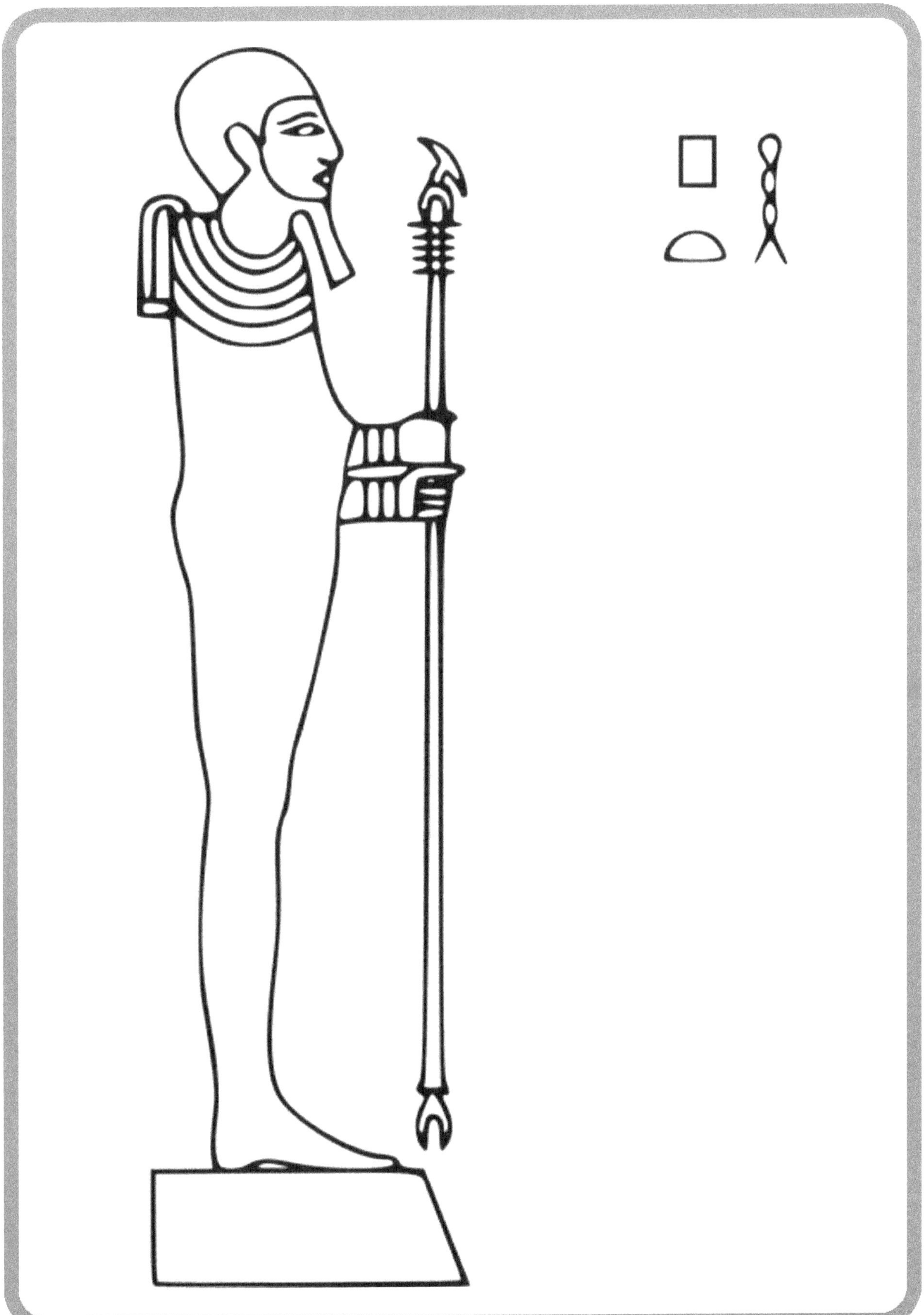

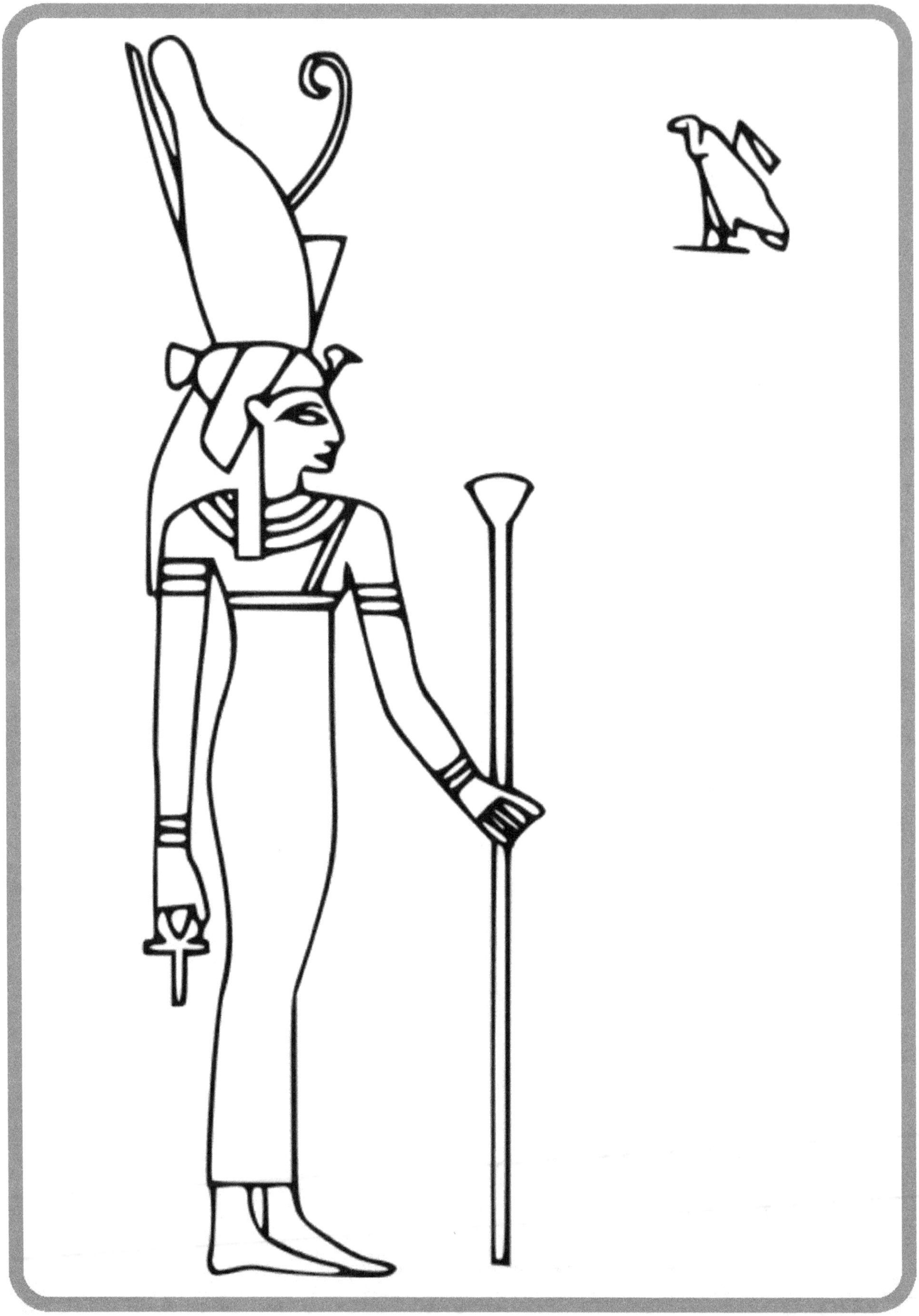

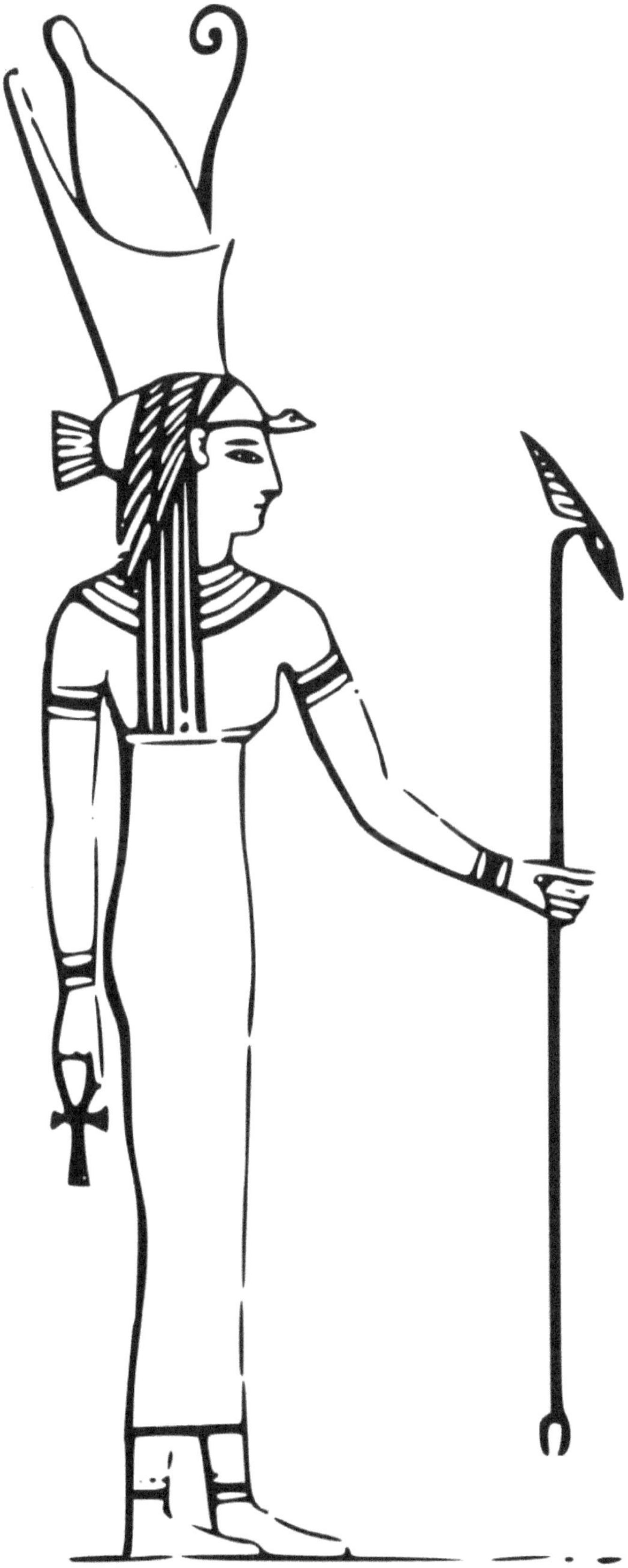

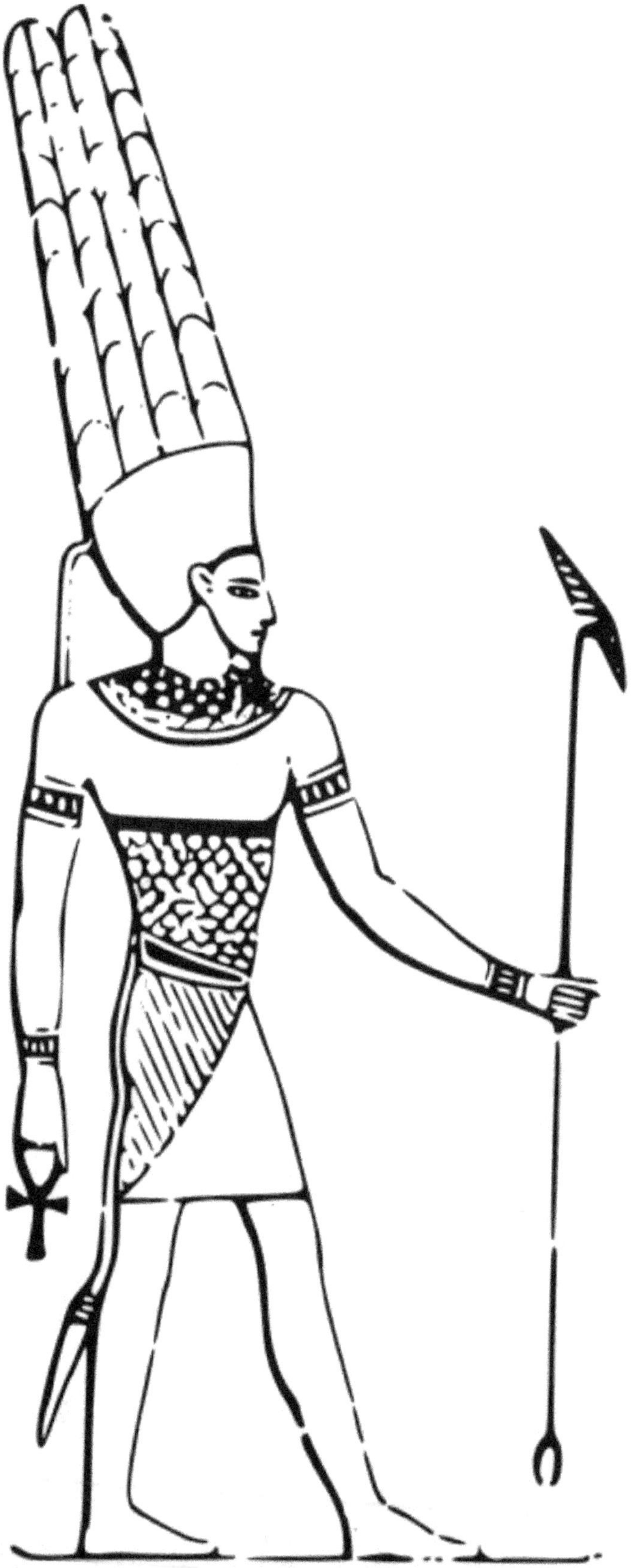

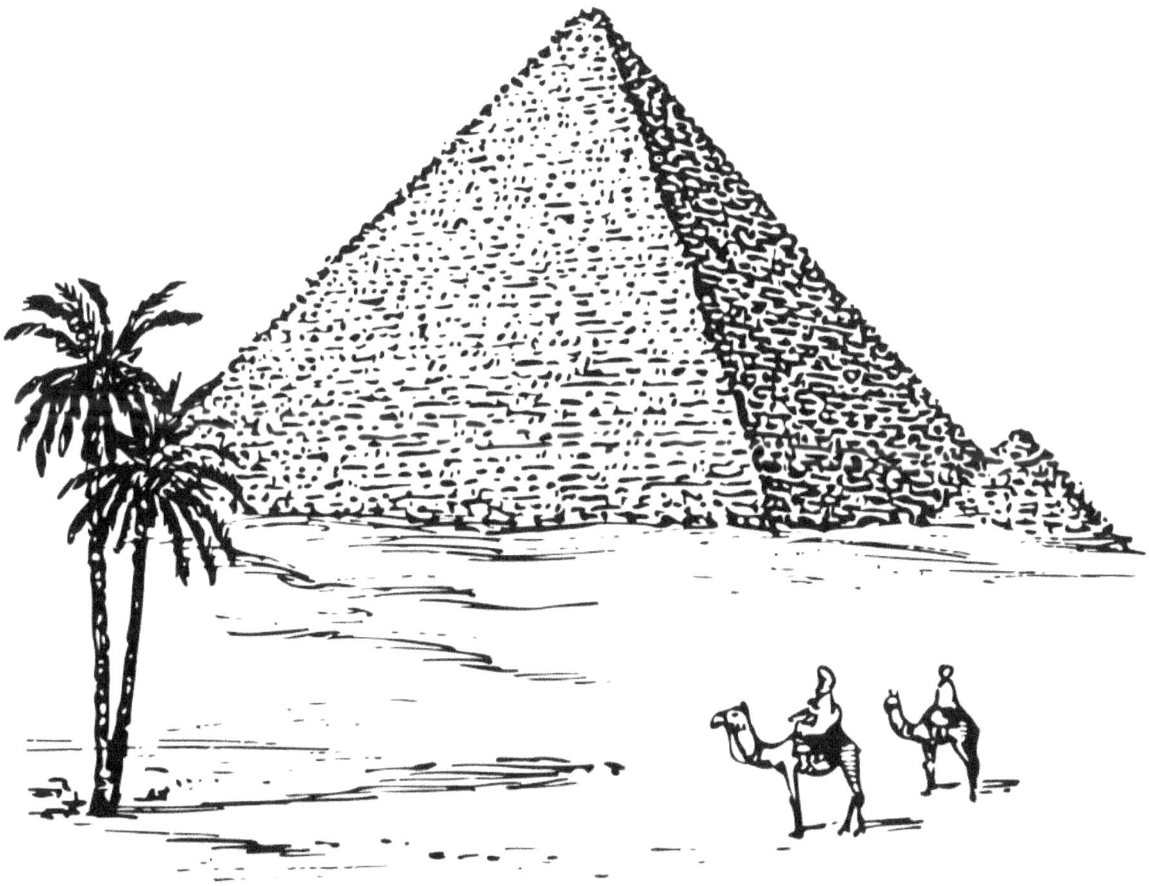

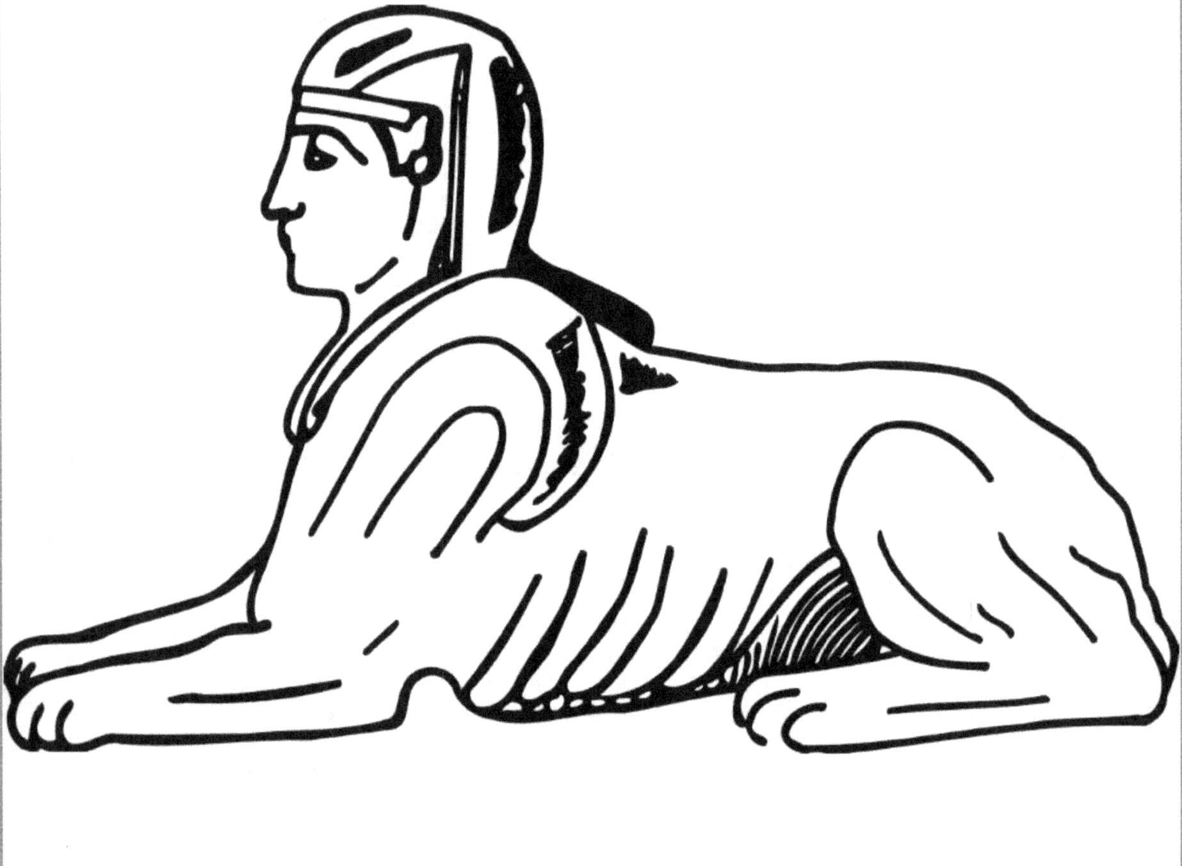

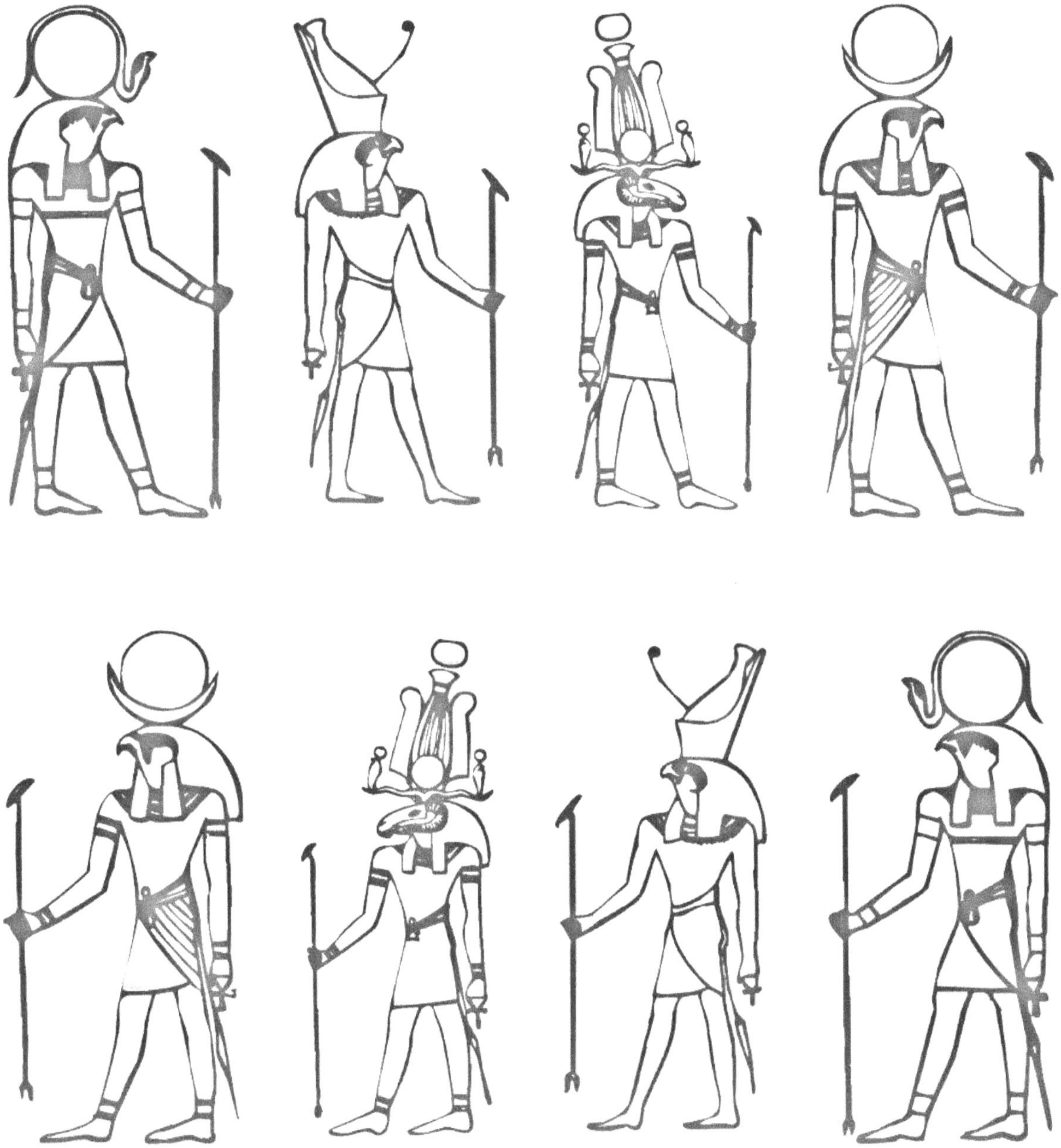

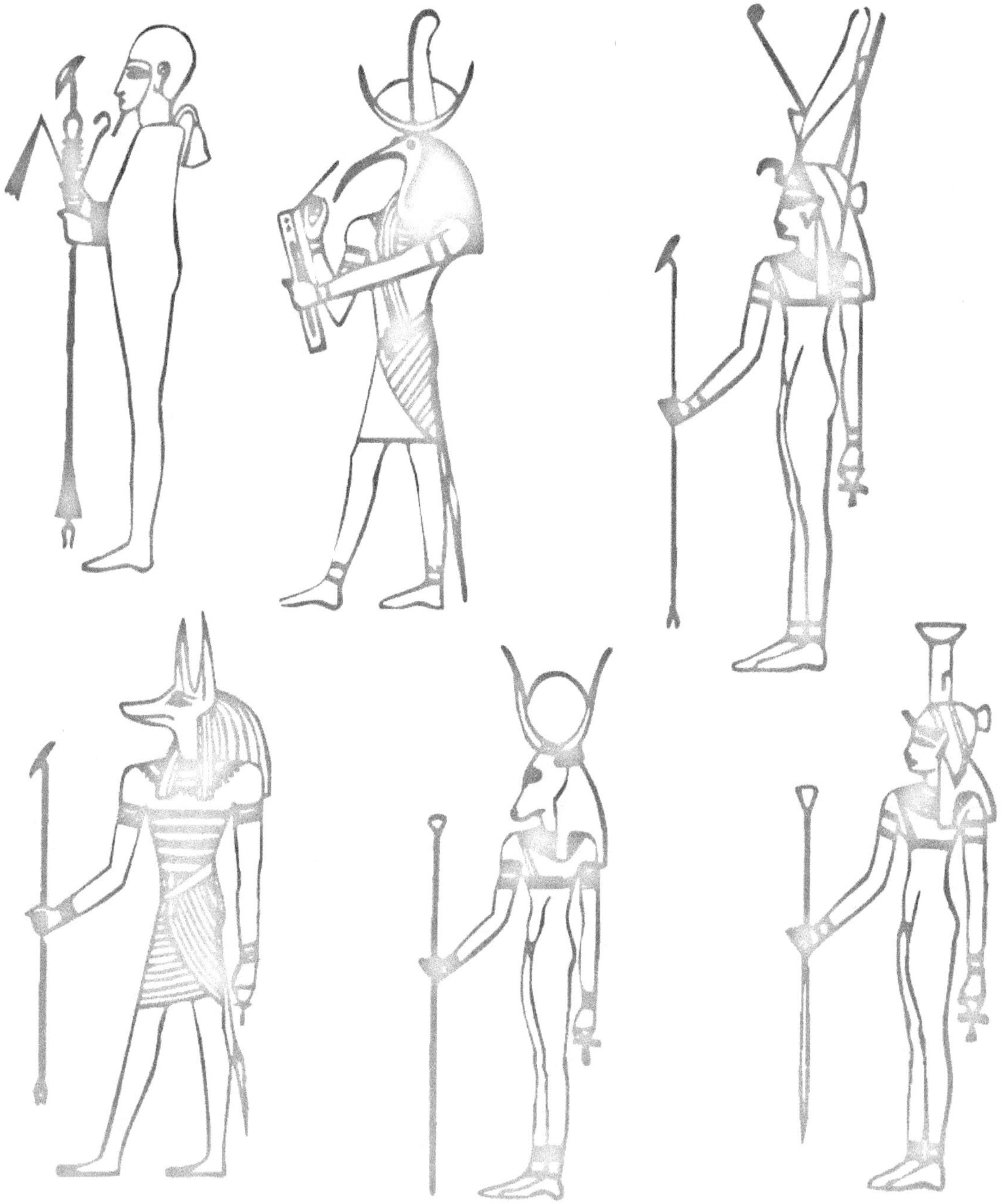

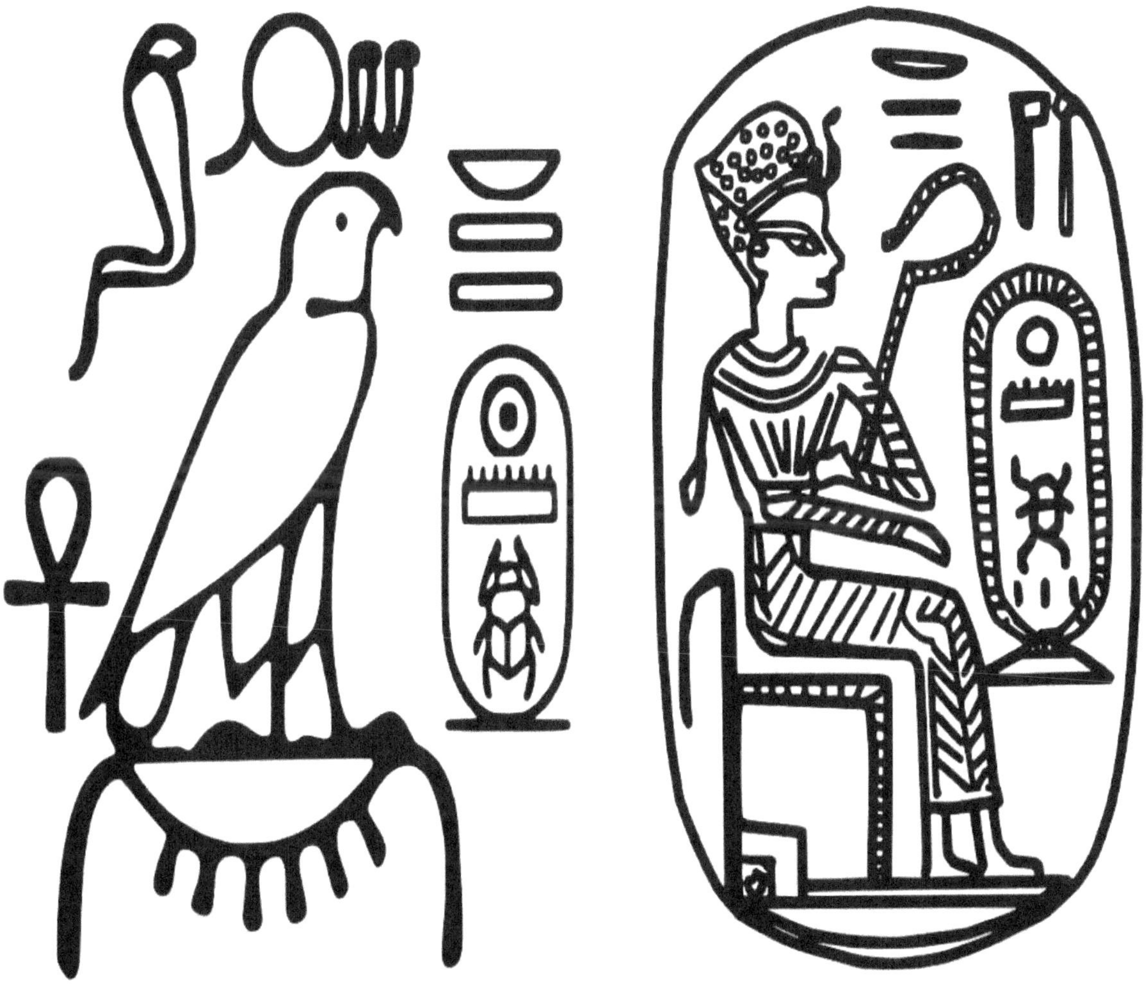

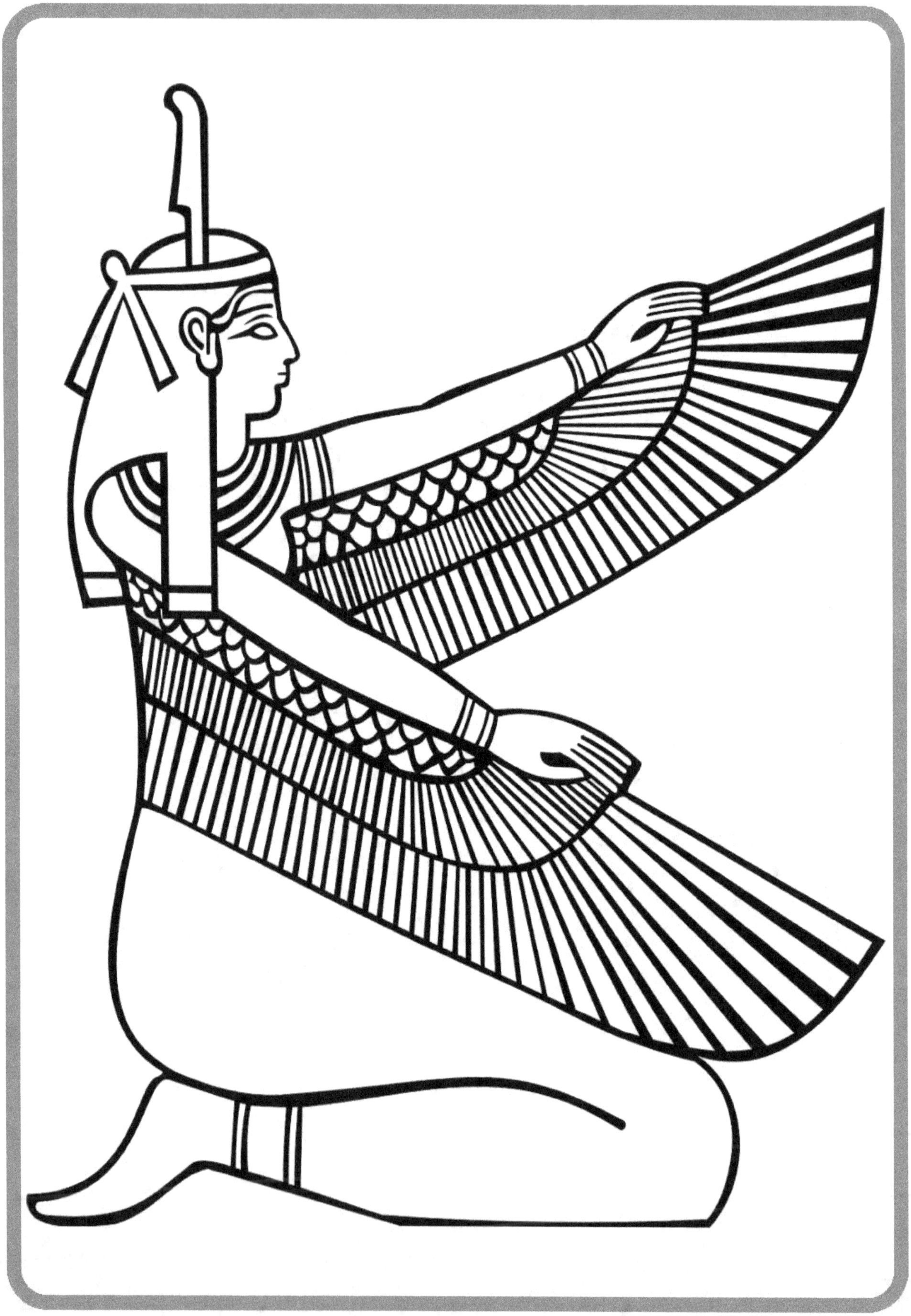

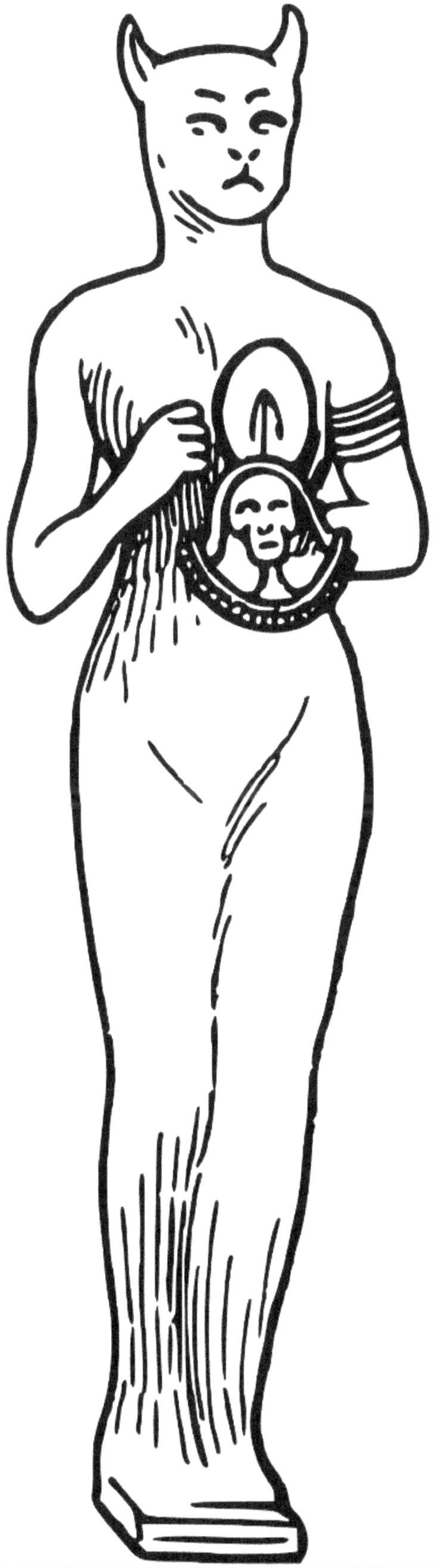

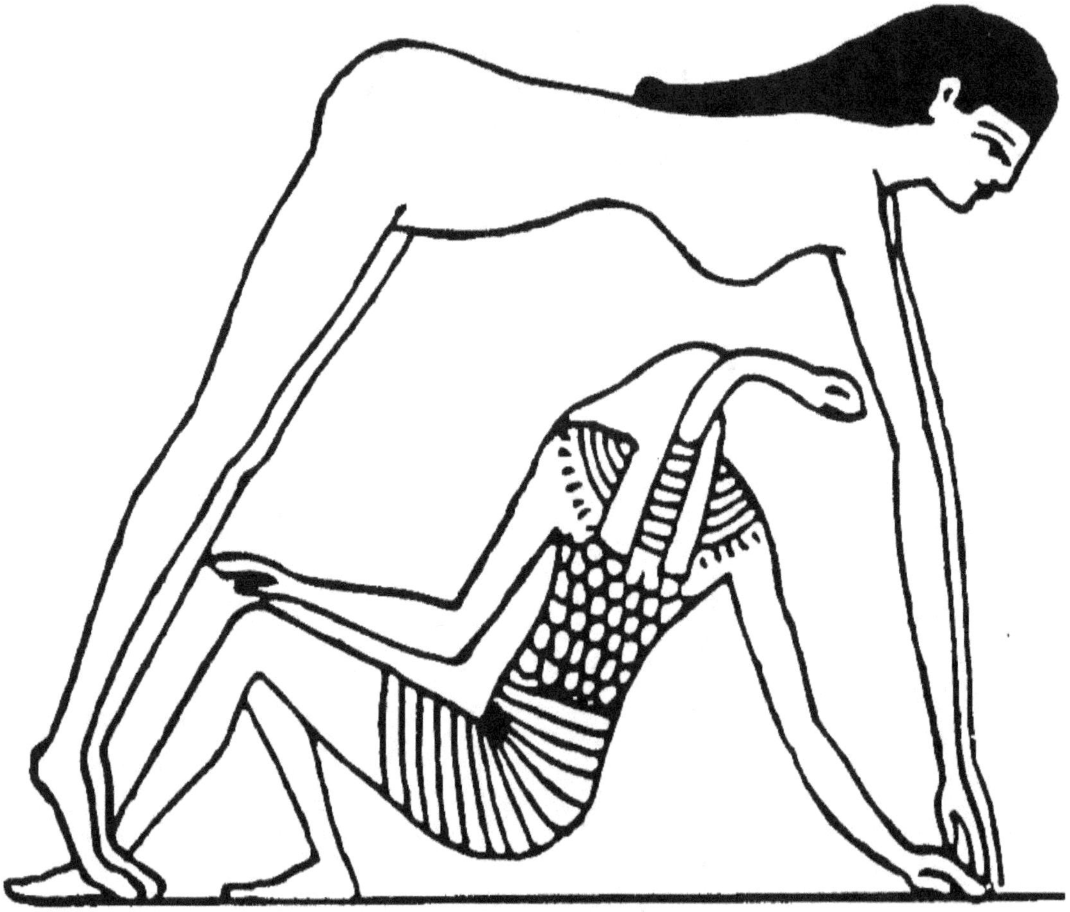

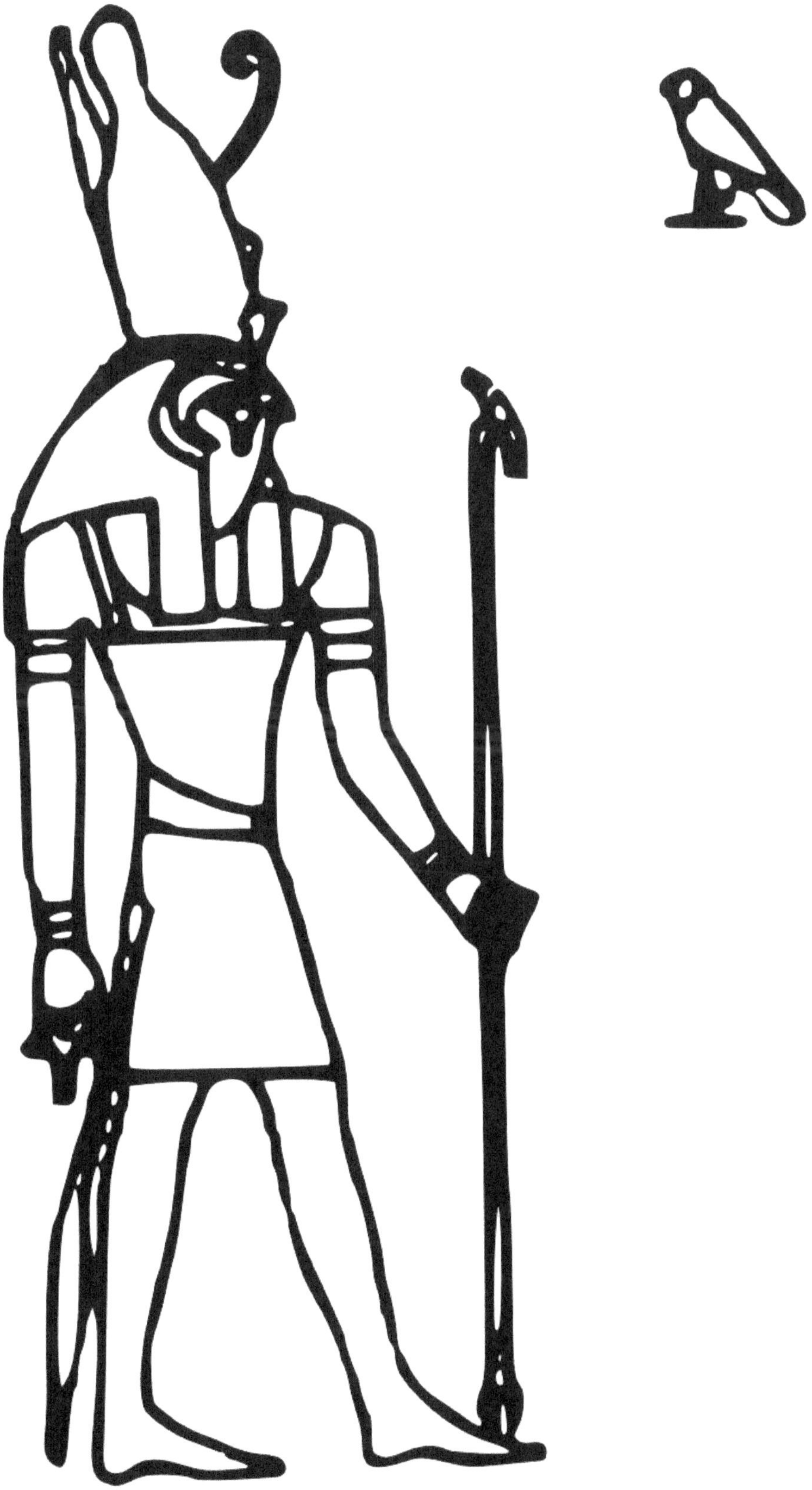

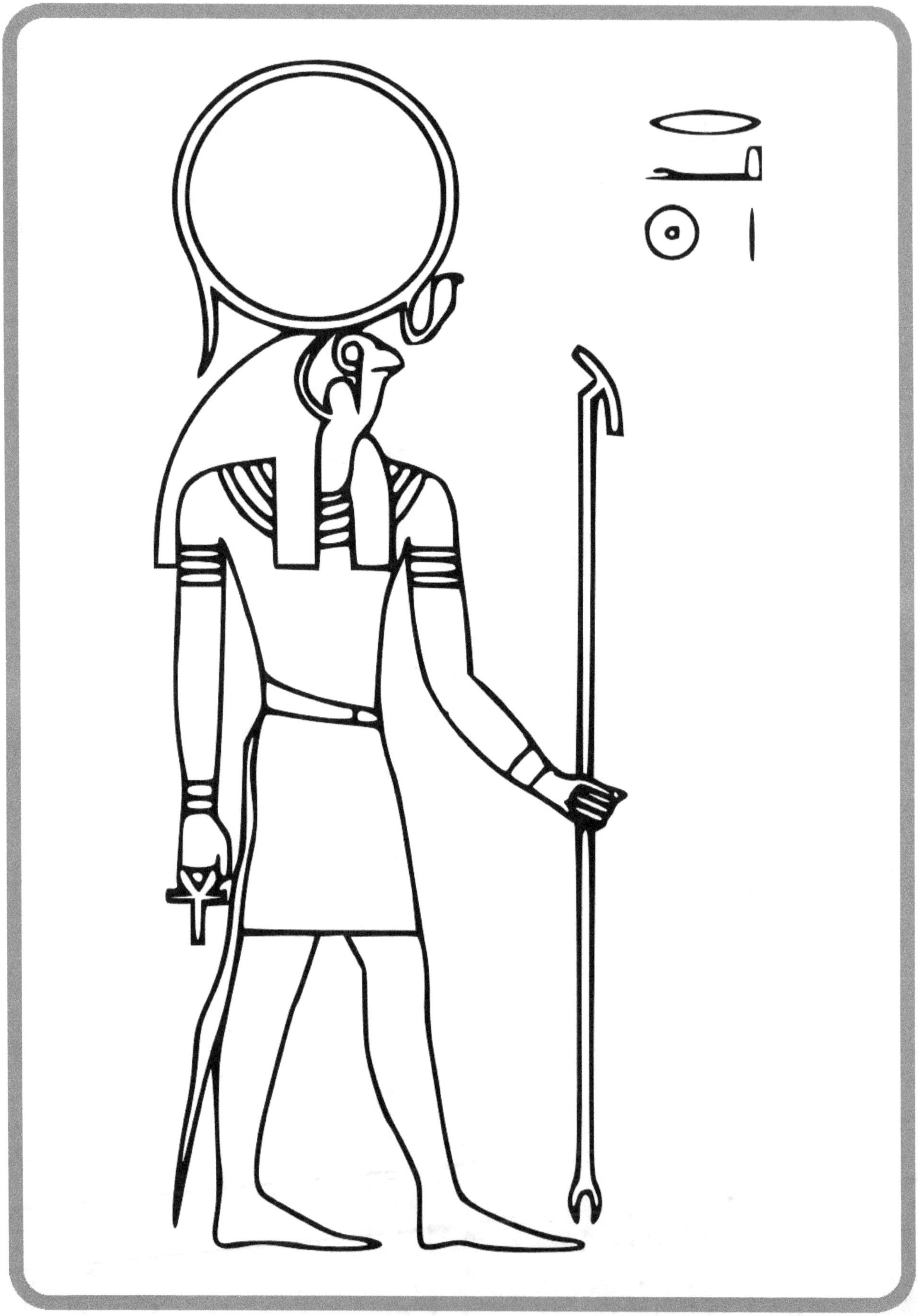

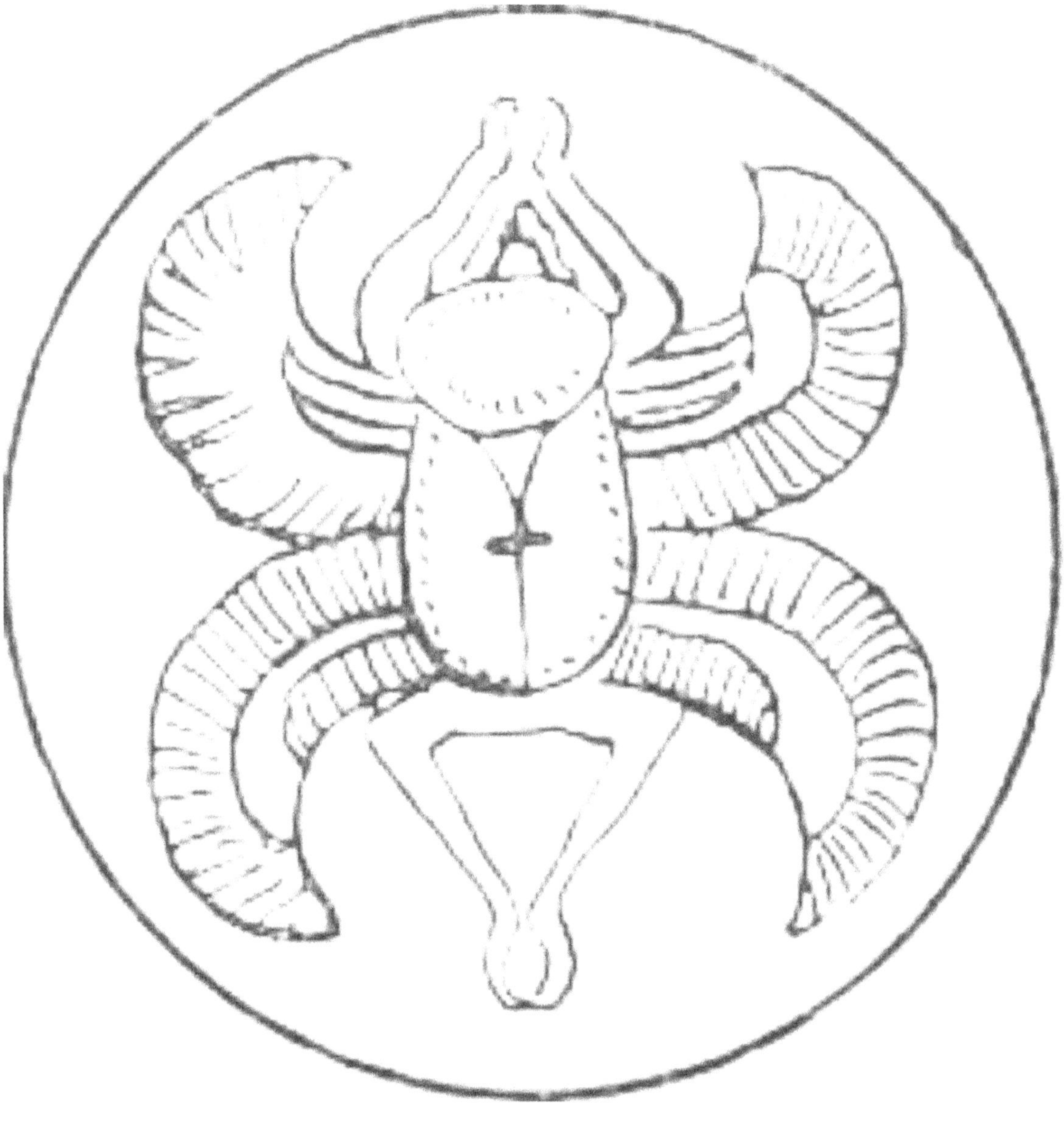

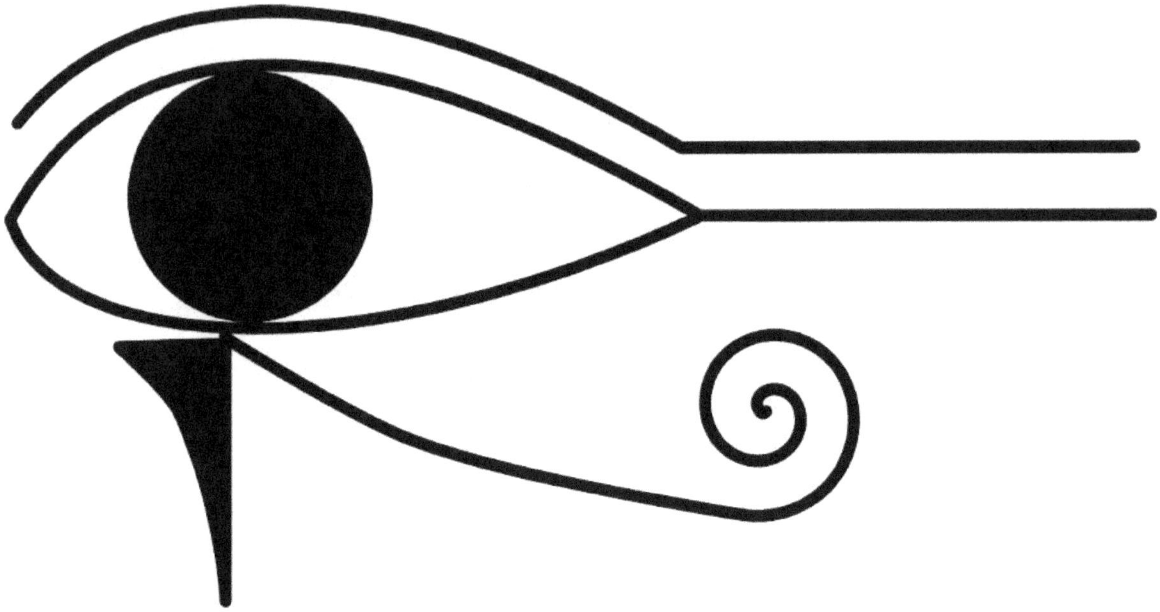

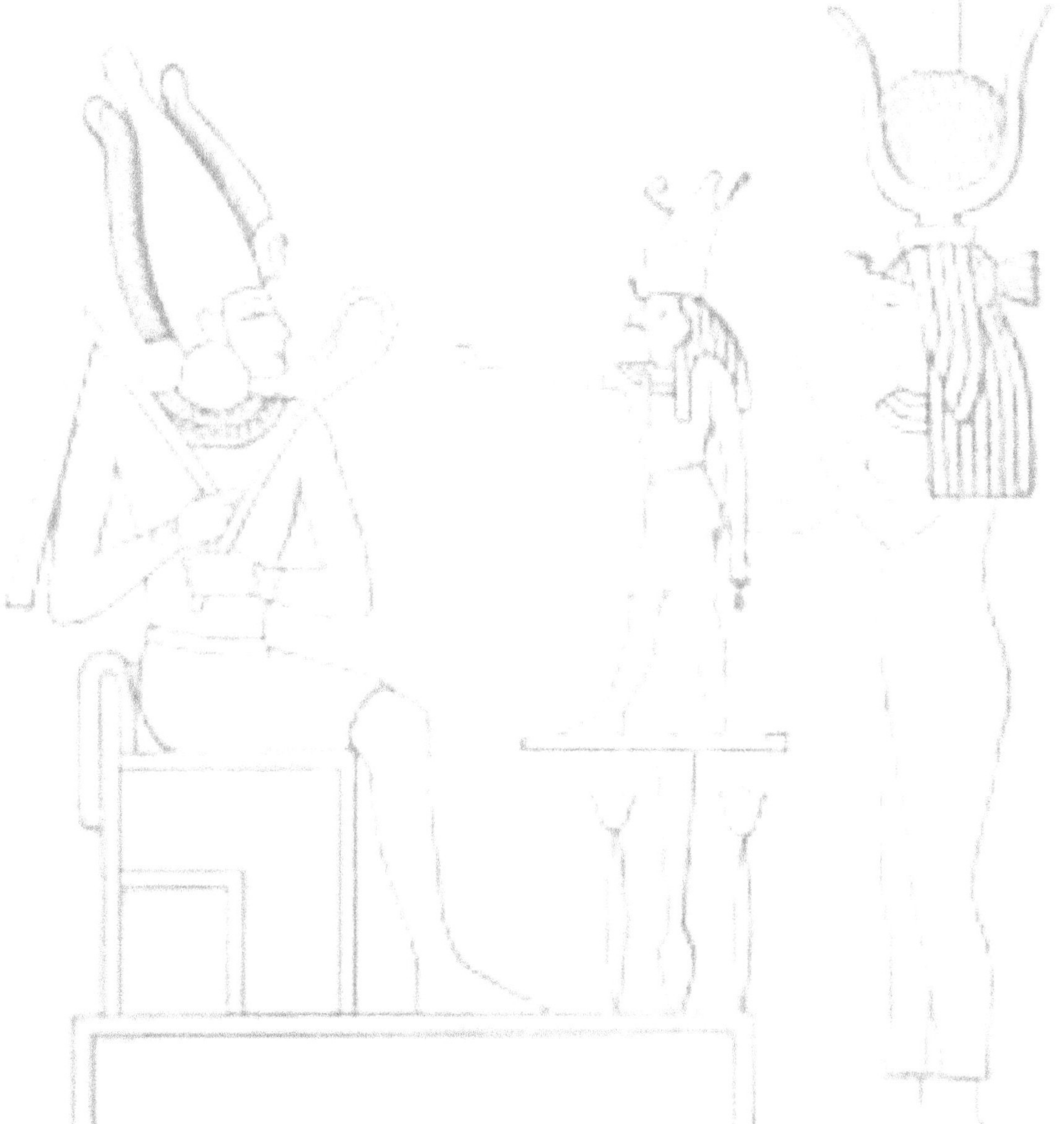

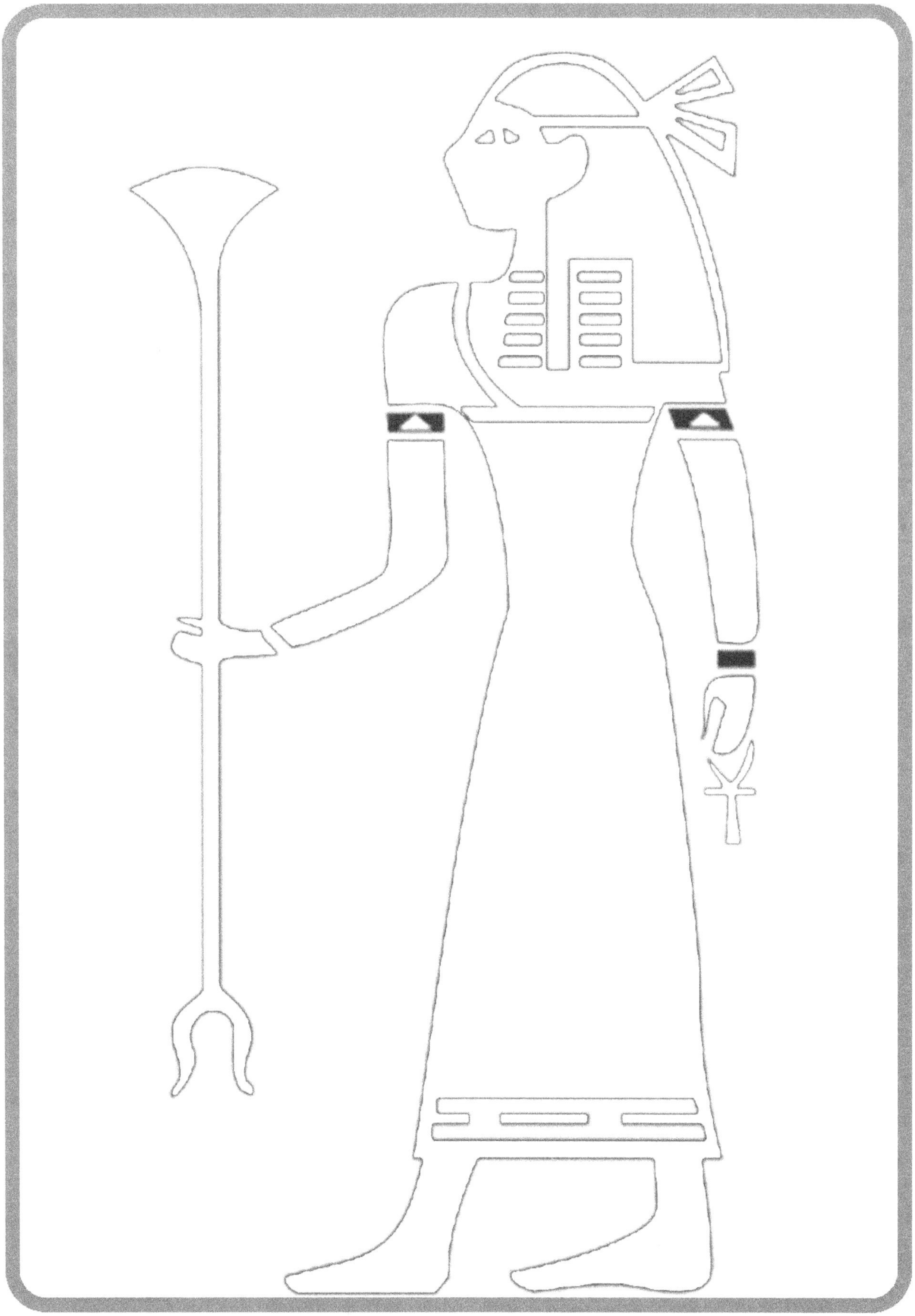

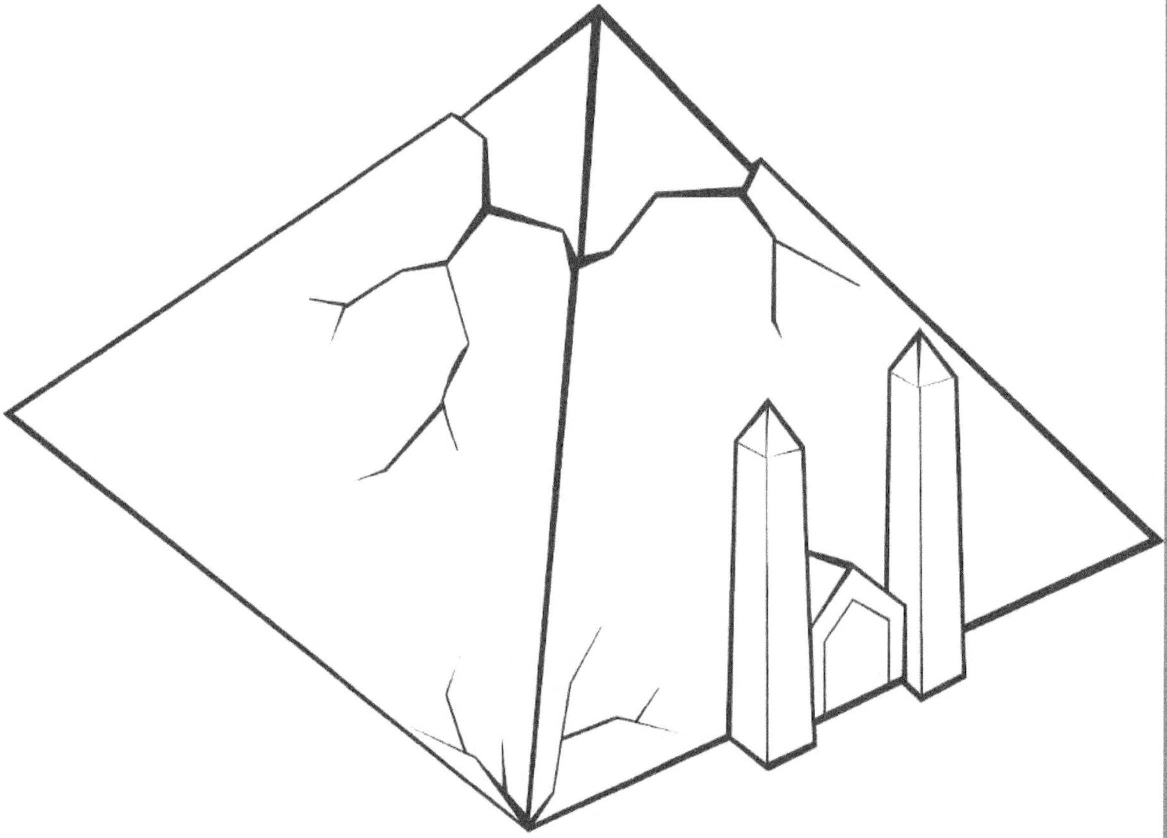

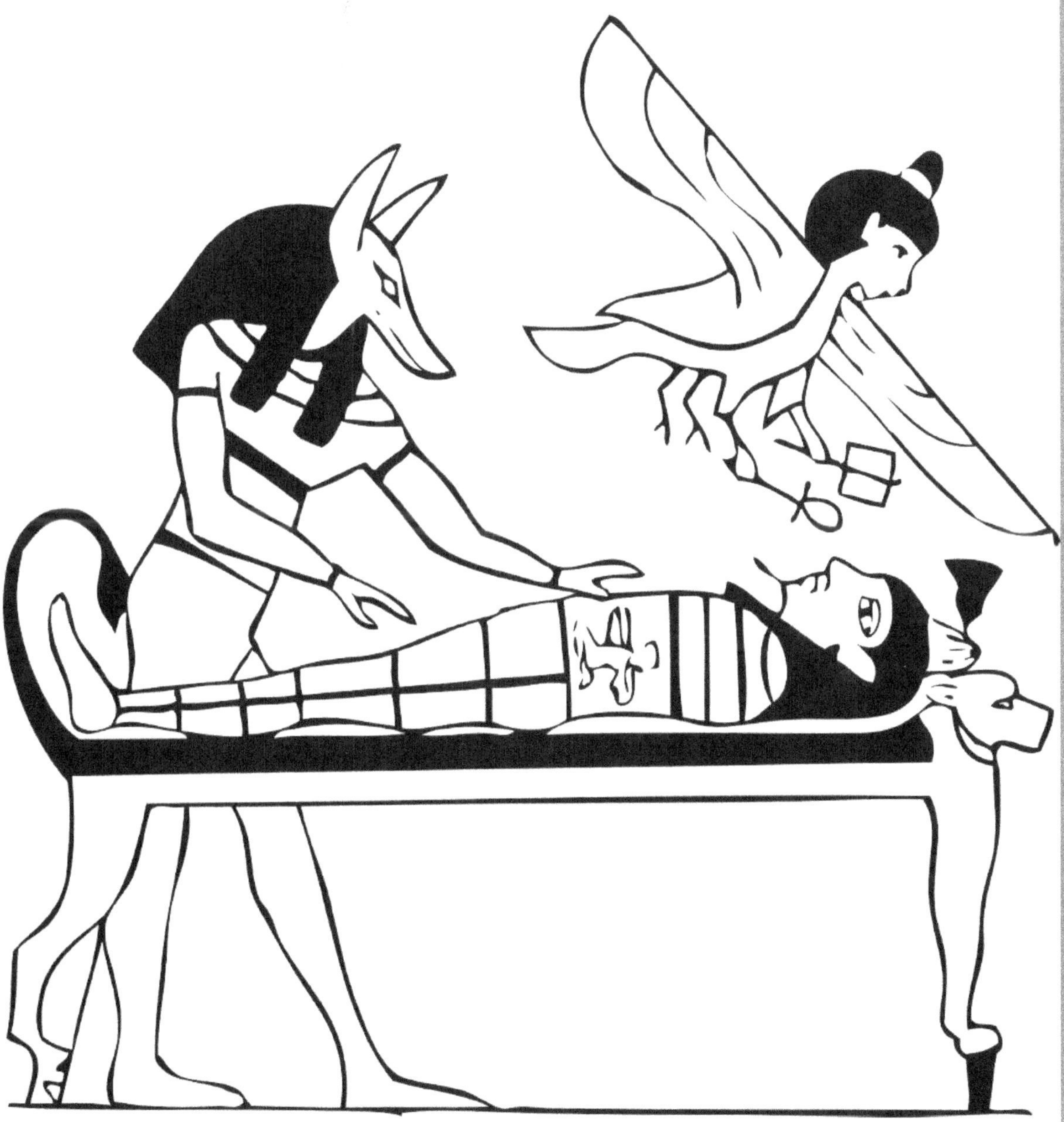

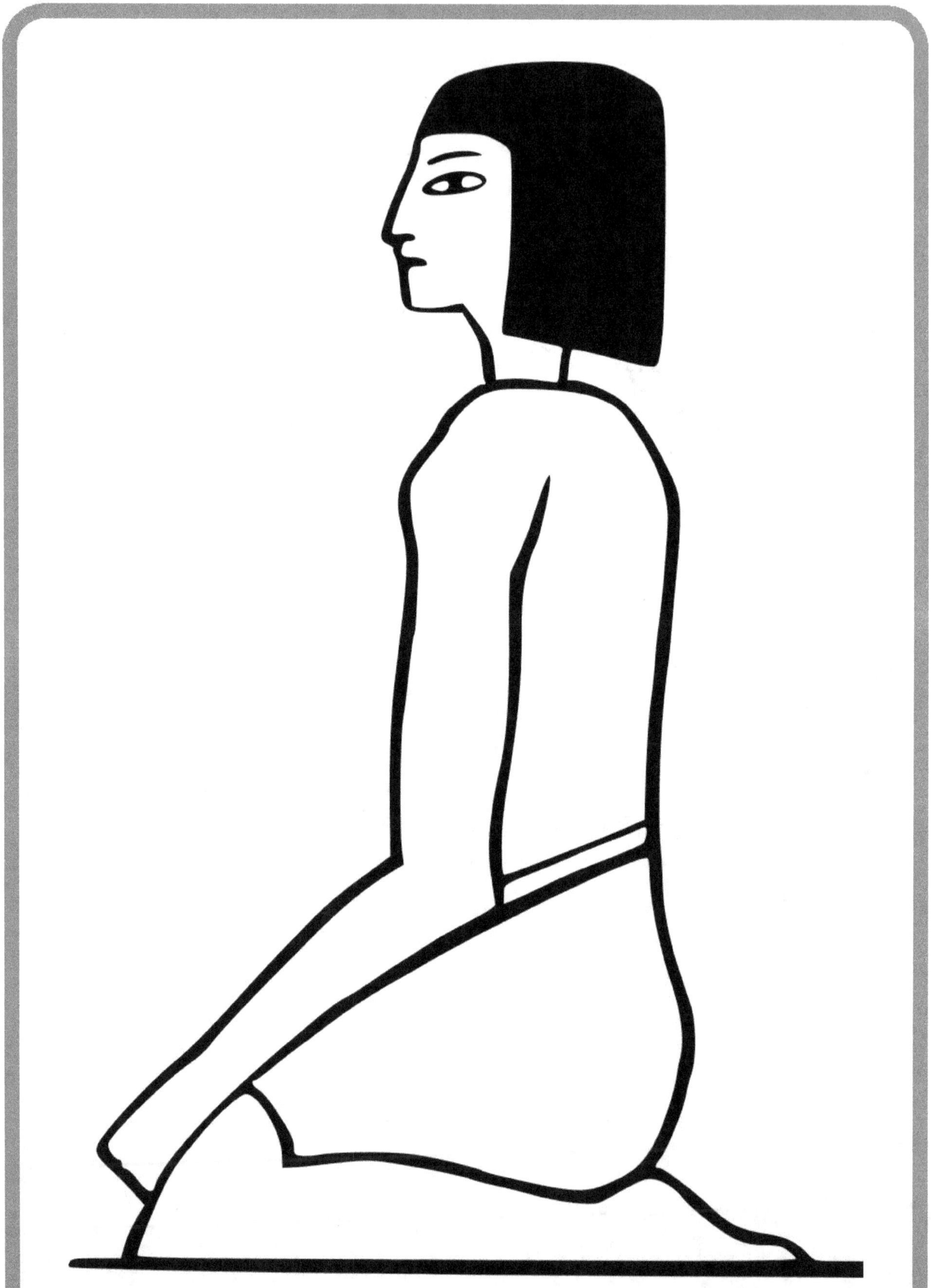

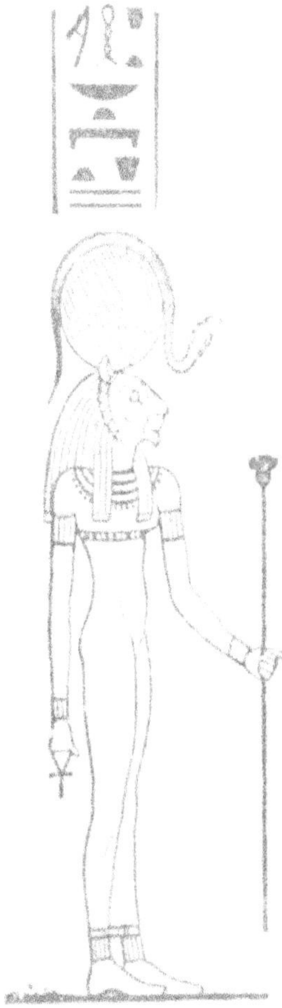

Sekhet Bast.

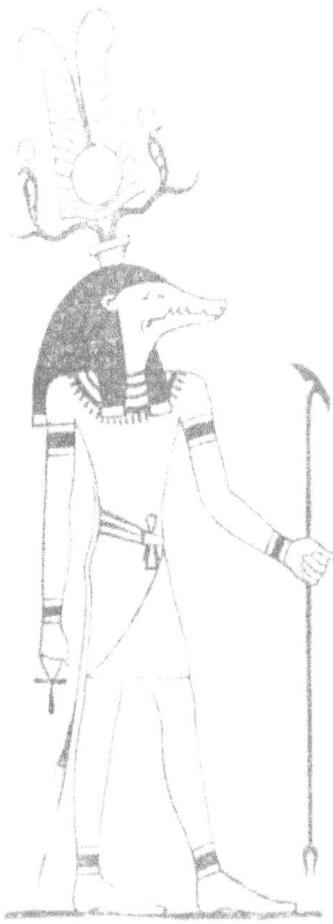

Sebek,

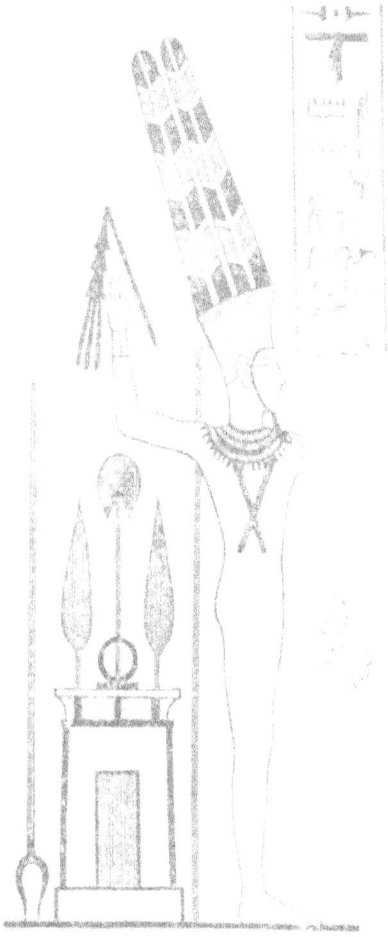

Khem Amun.

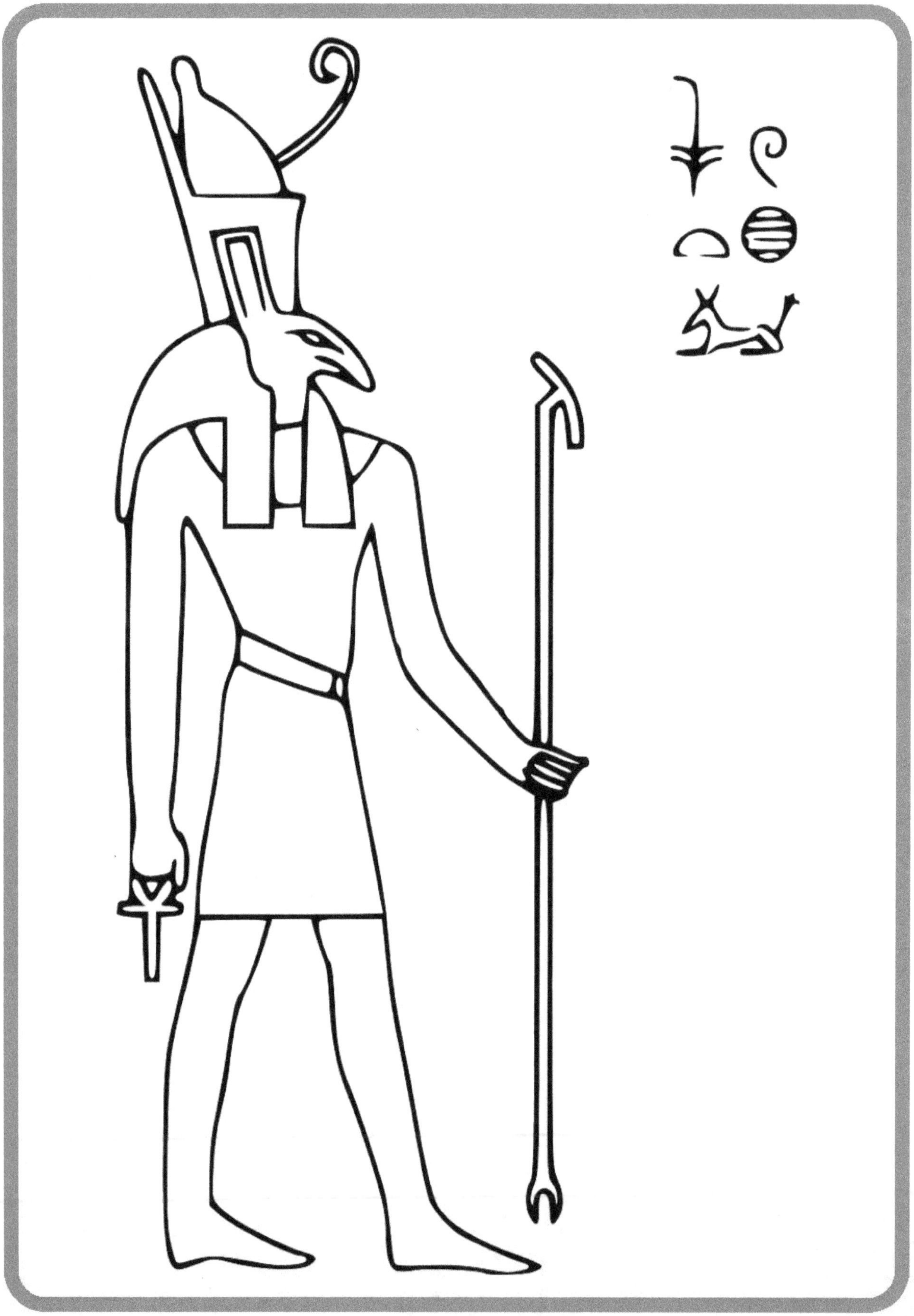

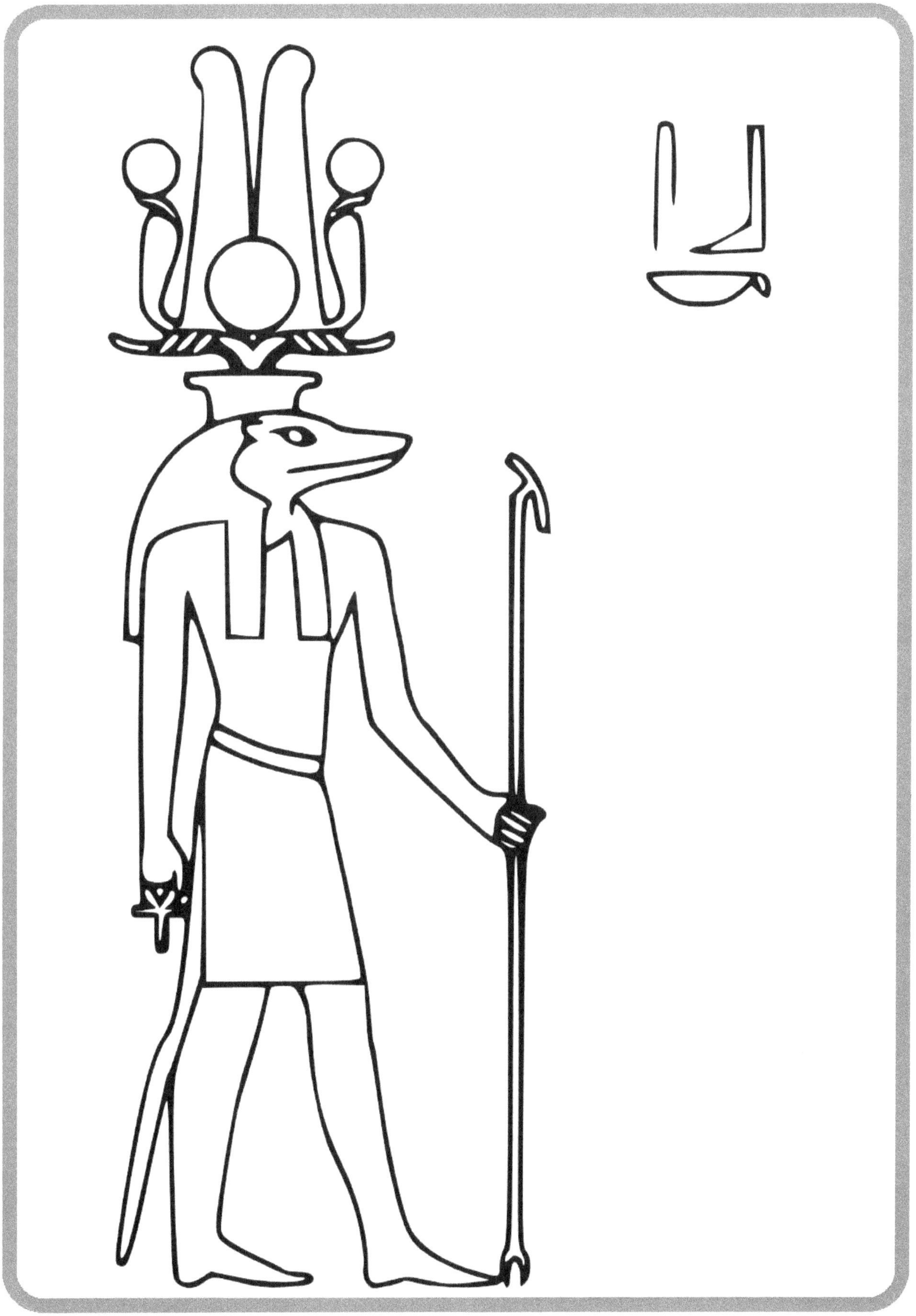

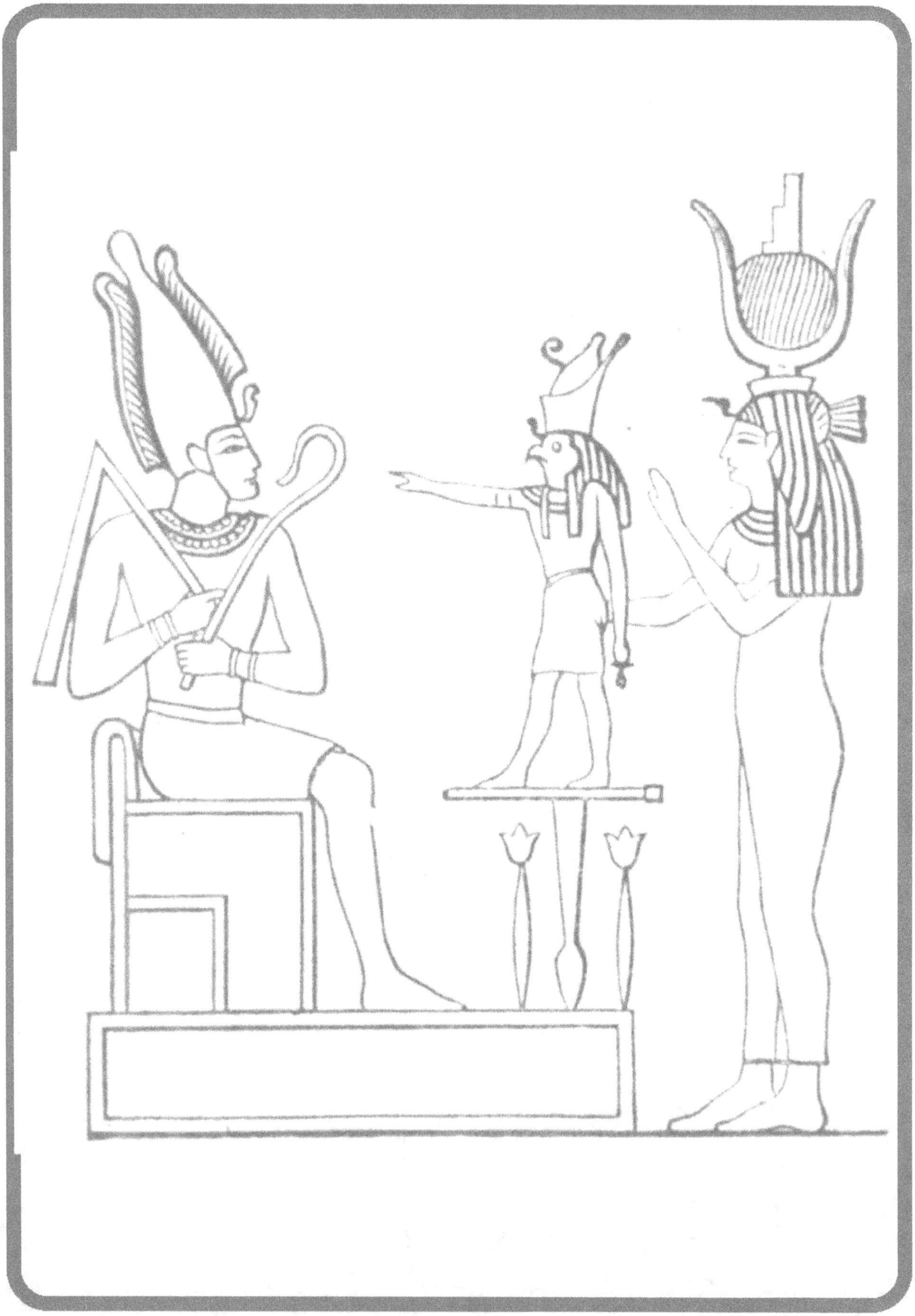

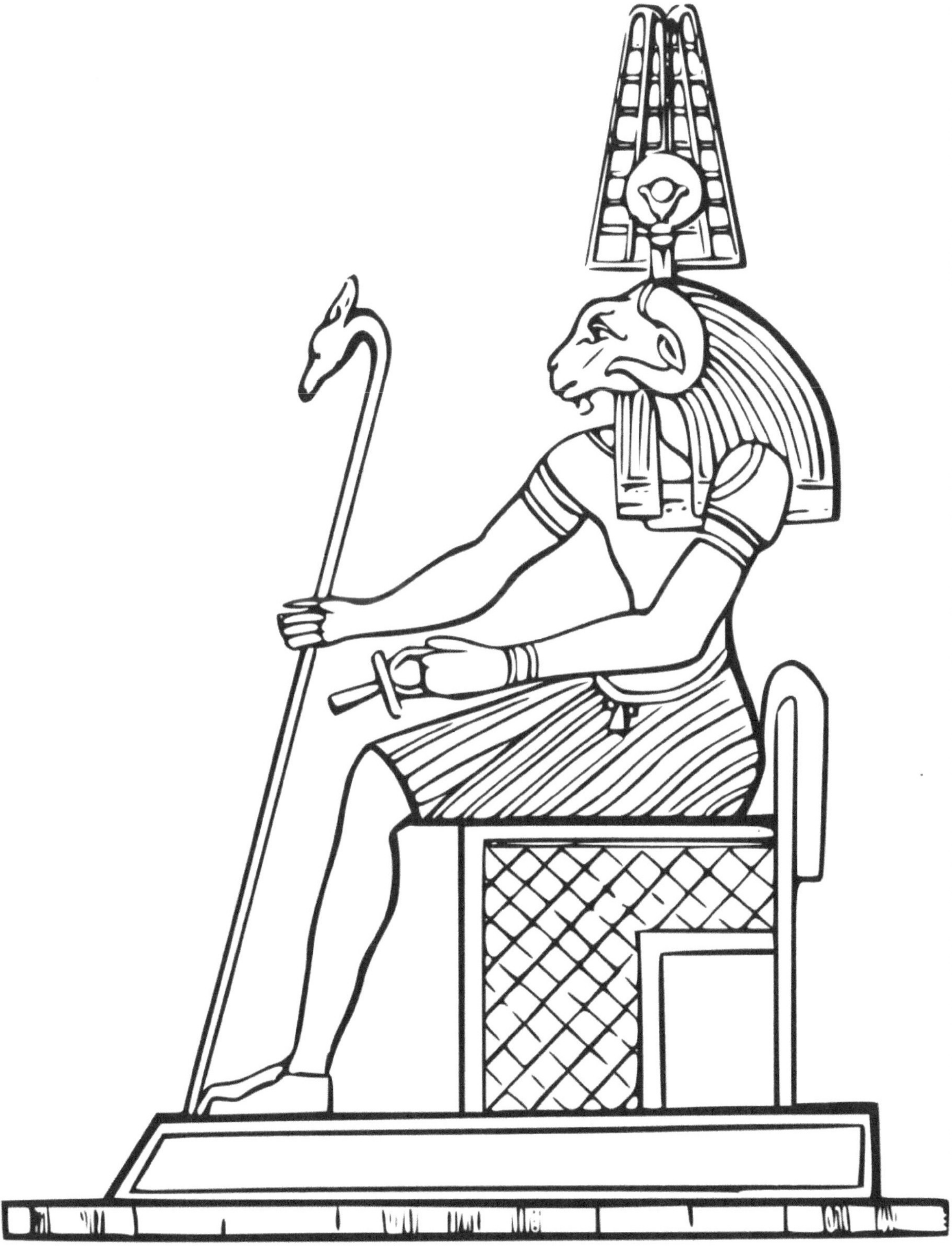

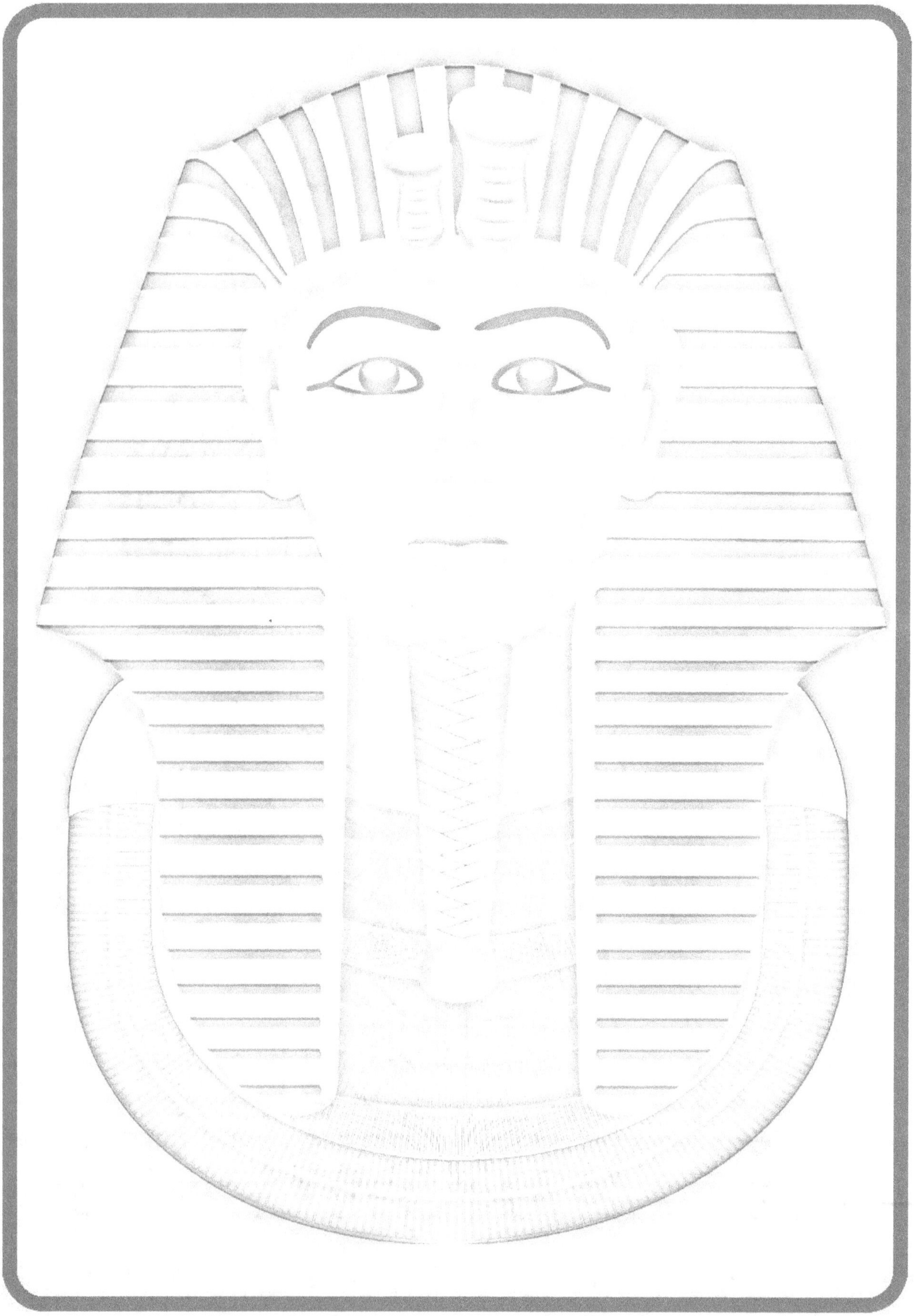

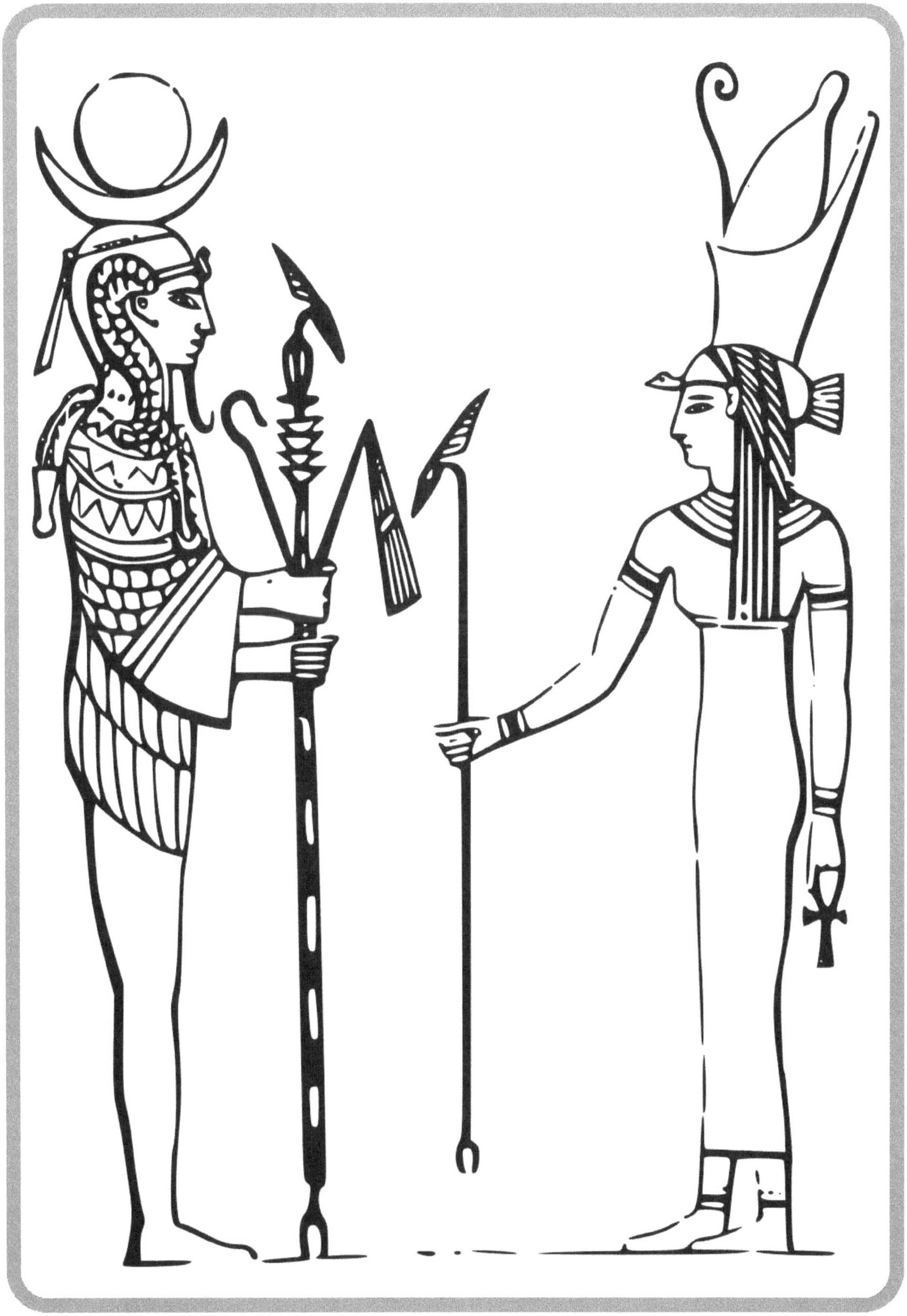

www.ingramcontent.com/pod-product-compliance
Lightning Source LLC
Chambersburg PA
CBHW062336220526
45469CB00008B/2730
9781730929717